CW00644653

Ex Libris
Name
Where
Date

THE CALEDONIAN

EDINBURGH

A Select Member of

THE MOST FAMOUS HOTELS IN THE WORLD

Caledonia

Caledonia, used in general somewhat loosely to denote the northern portion of Britain during the period of the Roman occupation of the island, had originally a more restricted application.

The word Caledonia is first met with in the fourth book of Pliny's Historia Naturalis *(ca 77AD), where, in the very meagre notice of Britain, the Caledonian forest (*Caledonia sylva*) is given as the northern boundary of the Roman part of the island. Its next appearance is in the* Agricola *of Tacitus (96AD) where Caledonia is unquestionably Britain north of the Firth of Forth.*

The etymology of the word Caledonia has been variously given. Celydd *(in Welsh a woody shelter) is the popular derivation; but Isaac Taylor (*Words and Places*) thinks the word may possibly contain the root* gael *and if so, the Caledonians would be the* Gaels *of the duns or hills.*

*Equally obscure are the ethnological relations of the people, the most probable opinion being that which regards as belonging to the British branch of the great Celtic family. A casual inference, hazarded by Tacitus (*Agricola*), that the red hair and large limbs of the inhabitants of Caledonia point clearly to a German origin, must not be pressed too far.*

Encyclopaedia Britannica, Ninth Edition, 1876

THE CALEDONIAN EDINBURGH

Andreas Augustin   Roddy Martine

Andreas Augustin
presents
THE CALEDONIAN EDINBURGH
in the series THE MOST FAMOUS HOTELS IN THE WORLD™

We would like to especially thank Dagmar Mühle, general manager of the Caledonian Hilton Edinburgh. She was the driving force behind this 'centennial project'.

It must be noted with greatest respect that the management of the hotel decided to accept historical facts rather than old legends and traditionally distributed myth.

We are in particular indebted to all former and current members of the staff, who contributed so generously to this book.

We would also like to thank Fiona Blair, Sarah Callaghan, Brydon Cunningham, John Dillon, Jorge Figuerola, Billy Garioch, Terry Gaughan, Selim Gecit, John Gibson, Gaynor Gillespie, Ann Graham, Ian Haggart, Marion Harvey, Jack Herkes, Margaret Jardine, Henry Klar, Ian Kruger, Moira Leggate, Jim Lindsay, David Lumsden, the Rt Hon Eric Milligan, David Nicol, Michael and Caroline Pearson, Andrew Penker, Mary Redden, Jimmy Reilly, Ena Robb, Stewart Scoular, Adrian Shaw, Andrew Smith, Helen Smith, A J Stewart, Eric Thorburn, Heather Warner, Rick Wilson and all the others who are not mentioned here by name.

Photographs: Archives of the Hotel, Famous Hotels Main Archives, Roddy Martine Collection, National Galleries of Scotland, The City Art Centre and the Hilton Creative Library. In a few cases we were unable to identify the copyright owner. Please contact us.

DTP Assistance: HC Artwoman Production: Harrison Dolittle

Editor: Francesca Brizi

Note for publishers and authors

All the photographs used in this book are available as high-quality digital files. Please contact the archives of THE MOST FAMOUS HOTELS IN THE WORLD (archives@famoushotels.org) and ask for these illustrations for your own publications. We will be happy to provide them for you.

Fax: +44-870-136-7435

e-mail: friend@famoushotels.org

or visit us at:

www.famoushotels.org

ISBN 3-902118-10-5

Design: Ramazotti Michelangelo

Welcome

Andreas Augustin *was born in Vienna and studied hotel management at Klessheim Castle, Salzburg, before he became a journalist and publisher.*

During the mid 1980s he laid the cornerstones for what was to become a unique library of hospitality: the series The Most Famous Hotels in the World – books about famous hotels – from The Raffles, Singapore, The Peninsula in Hong Kong, to The Savoy London and The Oriental in Bangkok. In cooperation with Roddy Martine he compiled this history of Edinburgh's famous hotel.

Roddy Martine *is certainly the most competent person to co-author the history of this Scottish institution. He was born in Kuching, Sarawak, of Scottish parentage, and educated in England and Scotland. He contributes on a regular basis to a wide range of newspapers and periodicals throughout the United Kingdom, and is the author of over twenty books.*

For this book he opened his own archives where he found a photograph of his first interview with Yehudi Menuhin in a Caledonian Suite.

He researched the history of Edinburgh's legendary grand old hotel, interviewed former members of the staff and came across some of the most peculiar stories and anecdotes. With his help we look behind the scenes of this famous Scottish entertainment business, called The Caledonian Hotel.

The old station.

TABLE OF CONTENTS

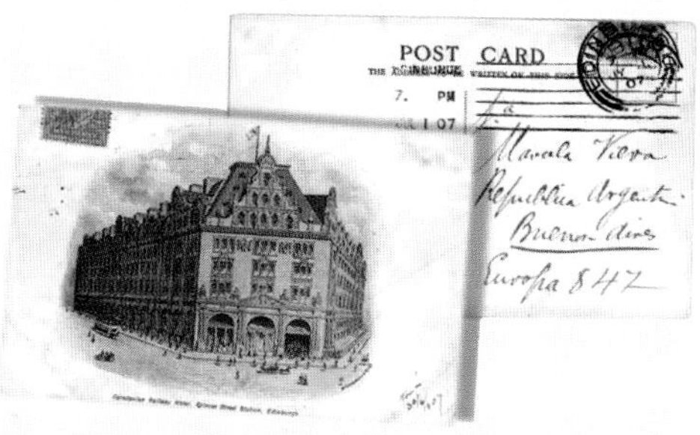

The first colour postcard of the hotel.

THE OLD TOWN . . .

Edinburgh, like Rome, is built on seven hills centred on an ancient volcanic rock which has had a castle upon its summit for over 1000 years. On the ridge of this rock, resembling a fishbone, the Old Town of Edinburgh travels east down the spine in the direction of the Royal Palace of Holyroodhouse which, in mediaeval times, lay outside the city gates.

In 1513, the Scottish army was dreadfully defeated at the Battle of Flodden, just over the border with England, and the Flodden Wall was flung up to protect Edinburgh from invasion by the English. The effect of this, however, was to encapsulate the Old Town of Edinburgh, and by the 18th century, with its overcrowded, vertical tenements, and an expanding population, there was simply no more room.

The decision was then taken to create a New Town in the fields to the north, which lay below the rock of Edinburgh Castle and the port of Leith, on the Firth of Forth.

The 'Building of the Royal Institution' by Alexander Nasmyth.

Henry Duguid (1831–1860), Edinburgh Castle from the Grassmarket

. . . AND THE NEW TOWN OF EDINBURGH

In 1767, architects and others were invited to enter a competition to create a New Town for the people of Edinburgh. Within three months a young architect, James Craig, was given the opportunity of his lifetime. The result is the magnificent World Heritage Site that we see today.

Much of Craig's triumph lay in the use of the site rather than in the originality of his plan. The exposure of Princes Street towards the high rise of the castle rock, with buildings on only one side, has made it one of the most picturesque shopping streets in the world. The North Loch, a protective mote which by the 18th century had become little more than the town sewer, was supplanted by Princes Street Gardens, and Craig's grid, occupied by elegant period houses, Georgian and Victorian, remains a lasting testament to good taste and refinement.

A pop-art digital media by Joplin Sinclair

For over 100 years the busiest place in the hotel: the lobby.

Traveller's Notepad

After checking-in at the Caledonian, I take a moment to enjoy the marvellous view over the valley across Princes Street Gardens; the old city to the right, the new city to the left. Through my window, in room 236, I can see the castle.

I quickly sneak out of the 'Caley', as the hotel is affectionately known in Edinburgh, and cross the road. I walk down the steps into St Cuthbert's churchyard. Suddenly the hustle and bustle of the city are far away, and I find myself steeped in the serene atmosphere of this historic graveyard. Buried here are the remains of George Meikle Kemp, who designed the Scott Monument on Princes Street, commemorating novelist Sir Walter Scott. Here, too, lies John Napier, the great mathematician, astronomer, poet and prodigious inventor. It is also the final resting place of Alexander Nasmyth (one of his paintings is shown on previous pages), artist, architect, bridge designer and inventor, and Thomas De Quincey, author and essayist.

My target lies a bit further into Princes Street Gardens. I am meeting Roddy Martine, my Scottish co-author, at Ross Fountain.

Architect John Dick Peddie had originally intended the fountain for the forecourt of the Caledonian Railway station. The fountain, originally designed as a centrepiece for the Paris Exhibition of 1867, still carries the maker's name – A Durenne, Maitre des Forges, Sommevocle, Haute Marne.

After the exhibition, the statue was purchased by Daniel Ross, an Edinburgh gunsmith, who intended to present it to his native city. At considerable personal cost, Ross had it shipped in 122 pieces to Leith, but when the towering montage of scantily-clad and naked young women was unveiled before the members of Edinburgh Town Council, they were horrified. It was all too suggestive and French; the sight of naked women in a railway station was too much for their prudish Victorian worthies. So the fountain ended up here, at a safe distance from the hotel. A perfect vantage point to tell the story of Edinburgh's famous landmark.

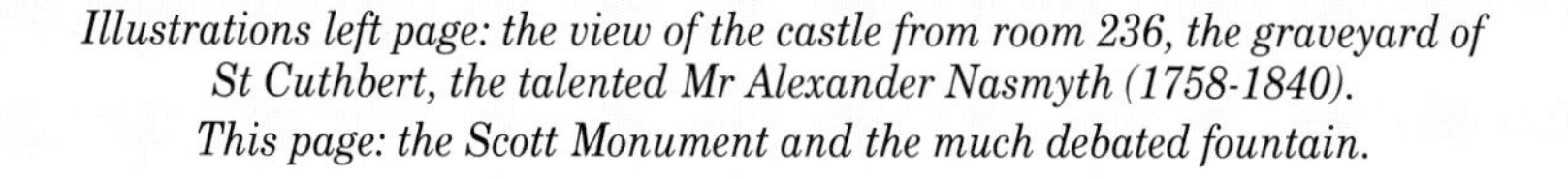

Illustrations left page: the view of the castle from room 236, the graveyard of St Cuthbert, the talented Mr Alexander Nasmyth (1758-1840). This page: the Scott Monument and the much debated fountain.

Caledonian chef Margarita Moreno is busy with dusting off a historic statue. Once a year members of staff participate in a local community initiative. This time it's cleaning parks to preserve Edinburgh's rich past. Let us join Margarita on her journey back in time to the days when the stage was set for a series of grand hotels that would make history.

Famous names had already made history. Scotland had become the land of artists and poets, engineers and inventors. Sir Henry Raeburn's portraits of the society figures of his day, including author Sir Walter Scott, geologist James Hutton, fiddler Niel Gow, mathematician John Playfair and philosophers Adam Ferguson and David Hume as well as the only recently discovered 'Skating Minister' graced the homes of Edinburgh's fine society. J W Turner, Alexander Nasmyth and Duguid had painted the city's most popular spots, poets had immortalized it and the world was about to discover the beauty of the Highlands.

The 18th Century New Town was dominated by the professional classes of law, medicine, finance and academia. The strong industrial sector (shipping, publishing, distilling and brewing) was largely relegated to the outskirts of the town, to Fountainbridge, to Granton, and to the nearby Port of Leith, not officially incorporated into the city boundaries until as late as 1920.

Sir Henry Raeburn (1756–1823): Reverend Robert Walker (1755–1808) 'The Skating Minister' Oil on canvas 30 x 25 inches. Owned by the National Gallery of Scotland, Edinburgh.*

On Scotland's West Coast, Glasgow, with its great shipyards on the River Clyde, was the major beneficiary of the Victorian Industrial Revolution to the extent of being designated the 'Second City of the Empire.' Collaborating with Edinburgh's astute financial expertise, both Edinburgh and Glasgow were prospering beyond their citizens' wildest dreams.

And against this background, and the accumulated wealth it created, came the railway network with companies competing fiercely to provide increasingly better services for their customers, especially between England and Scotland, and in linking Edinburgh with Glasgow.

In 1845, following an Act of Parliament, the Caledonian Railway Company was set up with an authorised capital of £2,800,000 to build 122¼ miles of track. Scottish landowner John Hope-Johnstone, Member of Parliament for Dumfriesshire, was appointed Chairman, and the Board of Directors comprised an additional 14 businessmen, seven from the Scottish Borders, the others from Glasgow, Edinburgh and London.

A link from Carlisle to Glasgow and Edinburgh over Beattock Summit in Dumfriesshire was long overdue, but would inevitably cause major disruption to remote local communities. Writing to a friend in August 1846, the learned author Thomas Carlisle observed that the main line north of Dumfries ran through his birthplace, the village of Ecclefechan: 'The harvest with its black potato fields, not great things, and all roads and lanes over-run with drunken nav-

---

* *Part of the tradition attached to the portrait is that the reverend Walker is skating on Duddingston Loch, which lies at the foot of Arthur's Seat, a plug of a former volcano, which dominates Edinburgh, just to the east of the city centre. Robert Walker was a member of the Royal Company of Archers in 1779 and their chaplain in 1798.*
This painting, virtually unknown prior to 1949, when it was purchased by the National Gallery of Scotland, has become one of the most famous paintings in the world and a symbol of the National Gallery.

vies; for our great Caledonian Railway passes in this direction, and all the world here, as everywhere, calculates on getting to Heaven by steam!'

There were also rivalries to consider, between the Caledonian Railway, the Glasgow & South Western Railway, and the North British Railway, with its east coast line on the southern shores of the Firth of Forth. To begin with, fortunately, the Caledonian Railway and the North British Railway were parties to traffic agreements entered into with their respective English allies, so they co-existed with each other in relative harmony.

The track of 'our great Caledonian Railway' led specifically from Carlisle to Glasgow, with a branch to Edinburgh from Carstairs. At a ceremony on 9 April 1847, the foundation stone for the company's Edinburgh station was laid by the 7th Duke of Atholl, Grand Master Mason of Scotland. This was called the Lothian Road Station and was sited 300 yards south of its eventual location. It was opposite today's Usher Hall which opened in 1914, a gift from Andrew Usher, patriarch of the prominent Scotch whisky blending family of the same name.

The laying of the station's foundation stone in 1847 was indeed a grand occasion for Edinburgh. In attendance were a detachment of dragoons, and the Lord Provost, Adam Black, the son of an Edinburgh builder who became publisher of the Edinburgh Review and, at one stage, the city's member of parliament. Included in the ceremony was the interment of a time capsule which contained a copy of *The Scotsman* newspaper for that day, several coins of the period, and a copy of the Act of Parliament of 1845 creating the Cal-

A 2-4-0 mixed traffic engine, built 1872.

edonian Railway Company. In his speech, the building's contractor, John Stephenson, observed that once built, the Caledonian Station would enable passengers to 'leave Edinburgh in the morning and dine in London the same day,' an almost inconceivable prospect at the time.

The trains, however, would certainly live up to expectations. The overnight expresses from Euston to Edinburgh and Glasgow were the fastest trains out of Carlisle. The first two early morning fliers leaving Carlisle at 5.35am served Edinburgh and the north, and had the very sharp allowance of 84 minutes for the 73.5 miles to Carstairs, compared with the 89 minutes booked for the famous 8.13pm out of Carlisle, the afternoon 'corridor' train from Euston. However, in 1847, all that was in the future.

The Caledonian's directors were also convinced that Edinburgh would rapidly develop into a busy terminal station, and they were determined to build a prestigious hotel to accommodate visitors to Scotland's Capital, and those simply stopping off on their journey north into the Highlands and the North of Scotland – to Stirling, the Trossachs, Oban, Perth, Aberdeen and Inverness. Remember that this was the very same year that Queen Victoria acquired the lease of Balmoral Castle for her husband Prince Albert.

To meet this requirement, William Tite, designer of the Royal Exchange in London, was asked to prepare plans for an elegant colonnaded building fronting south onto Lothian Road. Then disaster struck. The Caledonian Railway Company ran out of funds and when the railway line connecting Edinburgh and London via Carstairs, Carlisle and the Midlands of England was finally completed on 15 February 1848, passengers had to make do with a temporary terminus, little more than an elongated shack in appearance. The hotel plans were put on hold and it was to be 20 years before a more personable station could even be contemplated.

Over those 20 years, both the railway company and Scotland, as a destination, took off. In 1868, John Dick Peddie, founder of the

THE INVENTORS

Scotland is basically everywhere; 61% of American Presidents have a Scottish ethnic background and inventions of Scots or people of Scottish origin have changed the course of history – from penicillin to television, the discovery of anaesthesia, the invention of the telephone and the theories of political economics.*

AN EXCERPT OF THE LONG LIST OF SCOTTISH INVENTORS:

James Napier (1550–1617) created logarithms.

Adam Smith (1723–1790): theories of political economics.

James Watt (1736–1819): separate condenser for steam engine.

John Loudon McAdam (1756–1836): road surfaces.

James Young Simpson (1811–1870): first use of chloroform.

James Young (1811–1883) manufactured paraffin wax and founded the mineral oil industry.

Kirkpatrick MacMillan (1813–1878): the bicycle.

James Clerk Maxwell (1831–1879): electricity & magnetism.

John Boyd Dunlop (1840–1921), a veterinary surgeon, invented the pneumatic tyre in 1889.

Alexander Graham Bell (1847–1922): the telephone.

Sir Alexander Fleming (1881–1955) discovered penicillin.

John Logie Baird (1888–1946) pioneered television.

Sir Robert Watson-Watt (1892–1973) developed radar.

More recently, Scottish scientists involved in genetic research at the Roslin Institute on the outskirts of Edinburgh were responsible for cloning Dolly the Sheep.

** Although the Scots comprise less than one-half of 1 percent of the world's population, 11 percent of all Nobel prizes have been awarded to Scotsmen.*

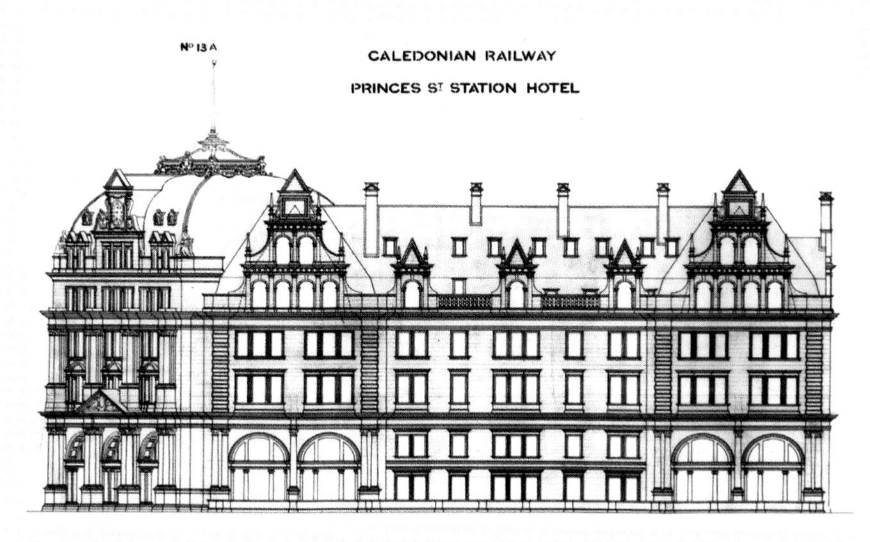

One of the original drawings for the hotel of John Dick Peddie dated 1868.

Edinburgh architectural firm of Peddie & Kinnear (still in existence – to this day, Peddie's designs are considered works of applied art. Literally dozens of them have survived including details for plaster ceiling centrepieces and patterns for wrought iron gates), was approached by the directors of the Caledonian Railway Company to design a new permanent station opening off the West End of Princes Street. The brief was also to include a large hotel to be built around and above the railway platforms. Then once again the company ran into financial difficulties and the plans were shelved. Instead, a new structure was erected facing Princes Street located opposite the watch tower built 41 years earlier in the corner of St Cuthbert's Churchyard to keep a look out for would-be grave robbers in the church's cemetery.

Twenty more years were to pass by until 16 June 1890, when fate took a hand in the situation, and the unloved little station pavilion was consumed by fire. In many ways, the timing could not have been better. The Forth Rail Bridge over the Firth of Forth was opening up. Flushed with the success and dividends of a thousand

The Aftermath of the Age of Enlightenment

Treasure Island - Sherlock Holmes - Harry Potter

Throughout a period that became known as The Scottish Enlightenment, starting towards the end of the 18th century and lasting well into the 1830s, Edinburgh provided some of the most stimulating minds in Europe. Philosopher David Hume, physician William Cullen, dramatist John Home, chemist Joseph Black, mathematician John Playfair, the first sociologist Adam Ferguson, philosopher Dugald Stewart and economist Adam Smith, author of the monumental *Wealth of Nations*. Great Scottish artists such as Henry Raeburn, Allan Ramsay and David Wilkie immortalised the intelligentsia in their portraits, while two generations of the Adam family of architects influenced the domestic lifestyles of the rich and famous throughout Britain. Frederic Chopin gave concerts in the elegant drawing rooms of the New Town, and crowds flocked to see the great actress Sarah Siddon's performance at the Theatre Royal which stood at the East End of Princes Street.

The literary giant Sir Walter Scott (1771–1832) was born into middle-class Edinburgh, and as a teenager was introduced to Robert Burns, Scotland's National Bard, feted by the Edinburgh intelligentsia. Robert Louis Stevenson was born in Howard Place, and grew up in Heriot Row before leaving Scotland to take up residence in Samoa. At Edinburgh University, he was a contemporary of Sir Arthur Conan Doyle (1859–1930), creator of the unforgettable Sherlock Holmes. Sir Compton Mackenzie (1883–1972), who wrote the classics *Monarch of the Glen* and *Whisky Galore*, moved to Edinburgh in the early 1960s, and in recent years there has been no scarcity of literary talent. *The Prime of Miss Jean Brodie* was written by Edinburgh-born Muriel Spark and based on her schooldays. Crime writer Ian Rankin has had considerable success with his Inspector Rebus novels, as has Allana Knight with her Inspector Faro books. Dorothy Dunnett (1923–2002) has a world audience with her House of Niccolo historic novels, and the first Harry Potters were penned by J K Rowling in an Edinburgh café.

'No place in the world can pretend to equal Edinburgh.'

Thomas Jefferson, Third President of America

THE 'TEMPORARY SOLUTIONS':

Top: Princes Street Station burnt down in 1890.
Below: the 'basement' of the Caledonian Hotel, the next temporary station solution until the hotel was built on top of it.

This Hamilton & Inches clock survived the station fire of 1890. It features today in Chisholm's Restaurant

miles of profitable track, the Caledonian Railway Company decided to invest for the future in Peddie's ambitious plans. Sadly, the great architect died in 1892 before the work on his masterpiece had even begun. His son, also John, took on the project and even, incredibly, managed a few improvements to his father's designs. Incidentally, the clock, which survived the station fire, can today be seen in Chisholm's Restaurant, still keeping perfect time, with occasional help from its original manufacturer, local company Hamilton & Inches in George Street.

The new Princes Street Station, with seven platforms leading north and west, was officially opened four years later, a few months before the Relief of Mafeking in the Boer War. By coincidence it was the very same year that the 5th Earl of Roseberry, whose ancestral home was at South Queensferry, became British prime minister, thus enabling him to arrive home for the weekends in style.

Edinburgh was now readily accessible from all parts of the United Kingdom. At the far end of Princes Street, operating out of Waverley Station, the North British Railway Company had already embarked upon building a huge hotel. The North British Hotel, today re-named the Balmoral Hotel, was completed a year ahead of the Caledonian Hotel, but although equally splendid, it was not on quite such a grand scale as its West End competitor. It is also interesting to note that despite fierce commercial rivalry between these two great

The Caledonian Railway triggered off a Caledonian Hotel-mania: The Aberdeen Caledonian opened in 1892, the one in Inverness in 1893.

The hotel under construction in 1900.

palaces of hospitality, a mutual respect rapidly developed between them. In the century that followed they often worked together, not least during the 1980s when, for a period, they came under the same ownership.

Although the go-ahead had been given in 1890, five years were to pass before building work began on the Caledonian Hotel, and it took a further four years to complete. The delay was worth it in the end. Even as a station, the edifice was inviting, with not one, not two, but three entrances under three great arches on its frontage. Once completed, the accommodation of the new grand hotel began to rise above them until Peddie's end relief for one of Europe's finest thoroughfares was finally completed.

On 21 December 1903, the citizens of Edinburgh gasped at the unmistakable opulence of their new acquisition, a 205-bedroom hotel of distinction to rival any comparable establishment anywhere in the world.

A SOCIAL STUDY

The original drawing of Princes Street Station Hotel – our Caledonian Hotel. Drawings of this nature are a social study of the period: there were only 1st class waiting rooms for gentlemen, but the ladies had 1st and 3rd class waiting rooms to ensure that servants were always close by. The lay-out of the ground floor rooms appears familiar: the 'Grill' has become the Castle Suite – the Ball Room (above), the staircase hall leads to the reception and even the revolving doors are still in place. Henry J Bean's can be found where the left luggage office was. Insets show first floor remains of the original station arches and the ground floor with Chisholm's Restaurant, featuring two original pink stone arches.

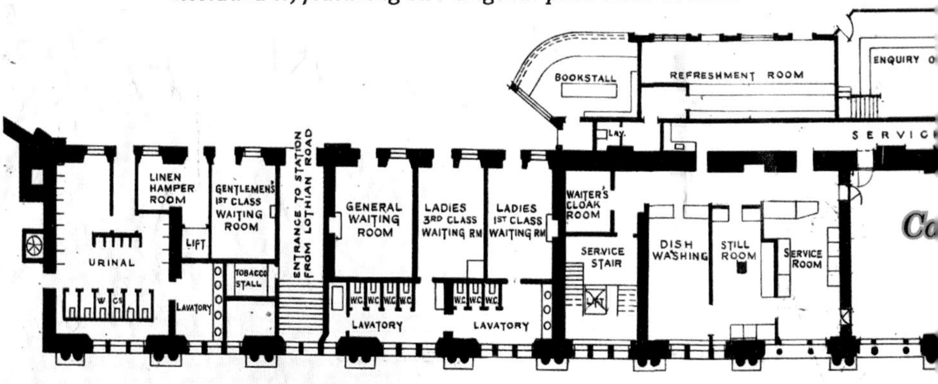

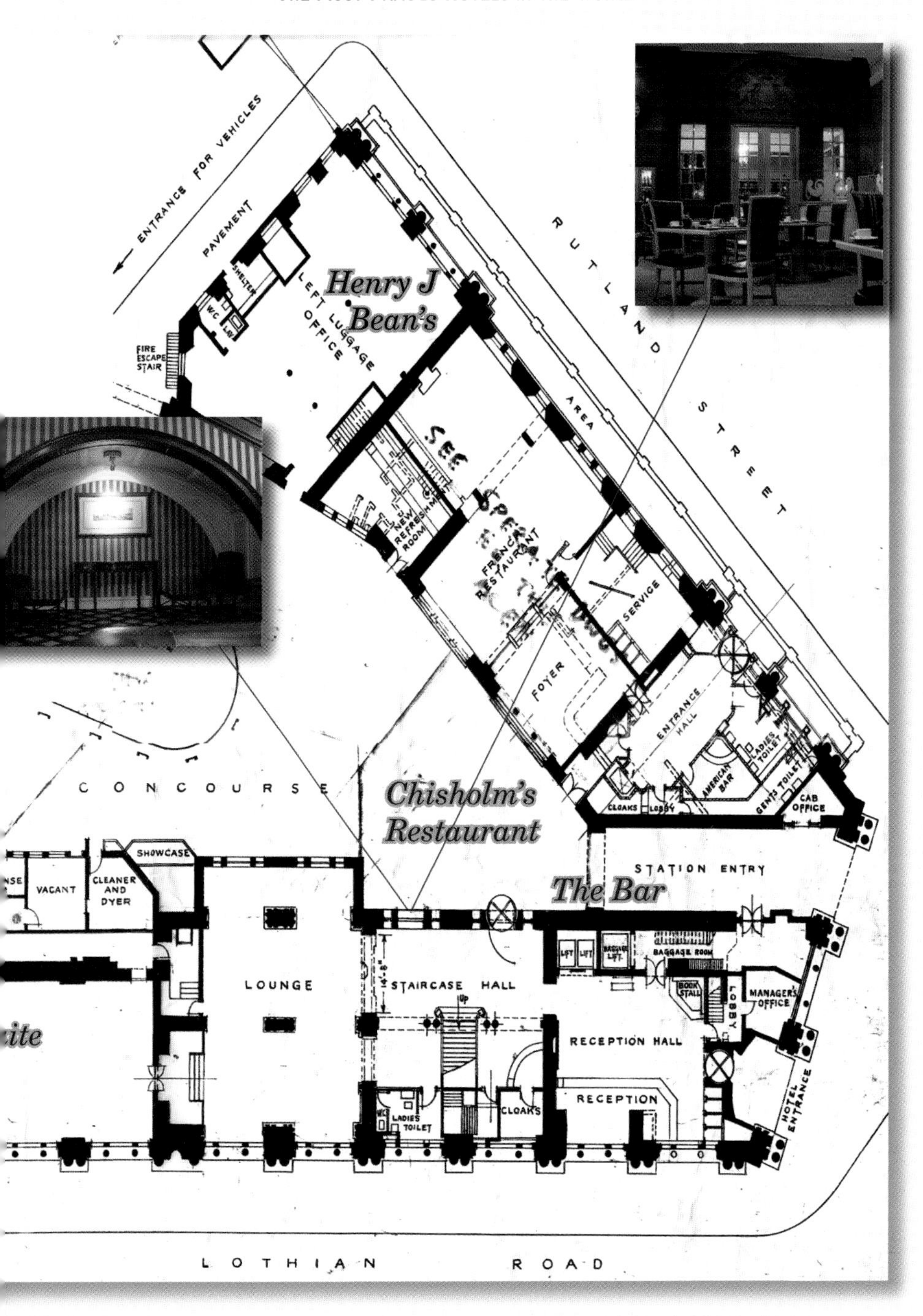

ENTRANCE FOR VEHICLES
PAVEMENT
SHELTER
FIRE ESCAPE STAIR
LEFT LUGGAGE OFFICE
Henry J Bean's
RUTLAND STREET
AREA
NEW REFRESHMENT ROOM
FRENCH RESTAURANT
SERVICE
FOYER
ENTRANCE HALL
AMERICAN BAR
LADIES TOILET
GENTS TOILET
CAB OFFICE
CLOAKS
LOBBY
CONCOURSE
Chisholm's Restaurant
STATION ENTRY
The Bar
SHOWCASE
VACANT
CLEANER AND DYER
LOUNGE
STAIRCASE HALL
UP
LIFT
BAGGAGE ROOM
BOOK STALL
MANAGER'S OFFICE
RECEPTION HALL
RECEPTION
CLOAKS
LADIES TOILET
HOTEL ENTRANCE
LOTHIAN ROAD

CALEDONIA
HOTEL ENTRANCE

Street life in front of the new hotel – the star of the West end.

The opening of the Princes Street Station Hotel, rapidly re-christened the Caledonian Station Hotel, helped to consolidate Scotland's position on the United Kingdom stage, then on the international stage, by heralding a new era of luxury and travel in Scotland. King Edward VII was on the throne of Great Britain and presided over the British Empire, not least as Emperor of India. Across the Atlantic Ocean, Theodore Roosevelt had become the 26th President of the United States of America following the assassination of President McKinley.

Scottish-born steel tycoon Andrew Carnegie was in the process of endowing public libraries and universities across the USA and Britain to raise levels of education. Engineer Henry Ford was busy founding a small motor vehicle company that would grow into a multi-national conglomerate, and the Wright Brothers had succeeded in keeping their latest invention in the air for a full minute before it touched the ground again.

In South Africa, the Boer War had recently ended. Russia and Japan were on the point of attacking each other, and Polish-born physicist Madame Marie Curie had just become the first woman to be awarded the Nobel Prize in recognition of her medical discoveries.

Nearer home, suffragette matriarch Emmeline Pankhurst had launched her Women's Social and Political Union, and yet another Scots politician, Arthur James Balfour, whose family home was at Haddington (eighteen miles east of Edinburgh) was in his second term as British prime minister.

Although Sir Harry Lauder, the great Scottish comedian, was already treading the boards at the start of his spectacular music hall career, the internationally popular songs of the day were 'Sweet Adeline', 'Shine on Harvest Moon', and 'Ida, Sweet as Apple Cider.' On the streets of Edinburgh there were horses and carriages, and horse-drawn buses. When out-of-doors, men wore flat caps, and gentlemen with top hats wore starched shirts with stiff collars and carried walking sticks. The ladies who accompanied them wore pavement-sweeping dresses with bustles, and magnificent fancy hats upon their heads.

However, Victorian values prevailed. Respectability was a key word. Appearances were everything. On Sunday mornings, the faithful were summoned to worship by the peeling of bells across the skyline. Observance of the Sabbath was sacrosanct for rich and poor alike, followed by the traditional family lunch, the one weekly occasion when everybody ate well (or as well as they could, depending upon their circumstances), and a brisk walk was likely to be taken in the afternoon.

In the Christmas of 1903, *Cinderella* was playing at the Theatre Royal at the east end of Princes Street, and Cook's Siberian Circus, 'The Greatest and Most Gigantic Show Ever Produced,' was pulling in the crowds at the Waverley Market.

Then on 21 December, an advertisement in *The Scotsman* newspaper announced that the Caledonian Railway Company's new hotel at Princes Street Station was 'NOW OPEN for the RECEPTION OF VISITORS.' Overnight, it was the talk of the town. Immediately across the road, Maule's Emporium – 'The Merriest Buying Place' cashed in on the event, hoping to boost its Christmas sales. The opening of this palatial hotel, it announced, made its West End location 'the pivot point on which all Edinburgh turns.'

The hotel with its large rose-coloured Permian sandstone façade quarried in Dumfries, dominated the skyline of the West End. The left-hand arch provided a pedestrian entrance to the hotel; the arch on the right-hand side led onto the railway platforms and into the railway's refreshment rooms. The new hotel's telegraphic address, 'Luxury Edinburgh', said it all.

Inside, the general public marvelled at the Pavonazzo marble hall with its gold painted ceiling, gilt-topped marble columns, and the sweeping staircase with its balustrade of marble and gilded wrought iron. Then there were the stained glass windows depicting the coats-of-arms of the major towns located upon the Caledonian Railway's network. For the people of Edinburgh, it was the beginning of an enduring love affair. The 'Caley', as it soon became widely known among Edinburgh folk, was the epitome of style and excellence. It was the tops.

And so much more. With the tall, imposing figure of its first general manager Alfred Tuke at the helm, the Princes Street Station Hotel became not only a landmark for the city, but a symbol of the very best of Scottish hospitality. So much so, that when the Caledonian Railway Company adopted as its logo the Scottish version of the Royal coat-of-arms – a prerogative hitherto enjoyed exclusively by the Royal Family – nobody said a word.

The original crest can be seen carved above the two inside doorways of Chisholm's Restaurant. These once led from the station into the hotel, and the crest can also be seen in relief at the front of the hotel alongside the coat-of-arms of the City of Edinburgh. Also featured at the front entrance are four modestly draped female figures symbolising Art, Commerce, Science and Agriculture, all of which relate to the ongoing prosperity of the great city which it serves.

CALEDONIAN RAILWAY

PRINCES S^{T} STATION HOTEL

DRAWING ROOM

ELEVATIO

A fine sample of the splendour of the interior design.

Close-ups

Classic Elements

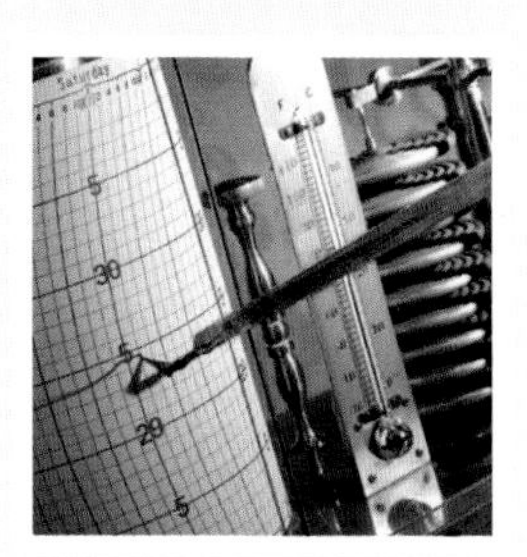

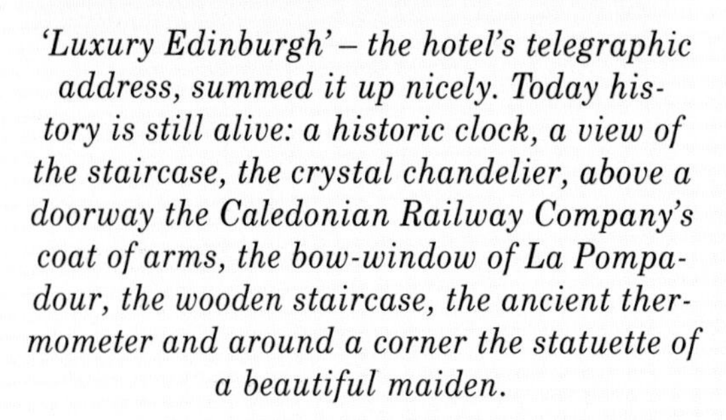

'Luxury Edinburgh' – the hotel's telegraphic address, summed it up nicely. Today history is still alive: a historic clock, a view of the staircase, the crystal chandelier, above a doorway the Caledonian Railway Company's coat of arms, the bow-window of La Pompadour, the wooden staircase, the ancient thermometer and around a corner the statuette of a beautiful maiden.

On 7 March 1904, a restaurant was opened on Princes Street Station to work with the hotel to provide lunches, dinners, teas and suppers, served at 'moderate charges.' This was the beginning of a reputation that in the decades to follow would lead to the Caledonian Hotel having one of the finest restaurants in Europe.

The Caledonian Railway trains were equally distinctive. The engine boilers and cabs were painted in a variety of shades of blue, with the lower halves in crimson red with black and white facings. Passenger carriages were a purple brown above, and white below. Gleaming, always immaculate, it was boasted by the owners that you could see your reflection in the engine surface.

Back at the Caley, Alfred Tuke assembled his staff with regimental precision. Soon, station posters began inviting the public to 'Come to the Caley' where they would be entertained 'with almost royal magnificence!' Rooms catered for reading, writing, billiards, private dining and 'late coffee.' One early report enthused that 'this hall and stairway might have been transferred bodily from the palace of a Venetian Doge!'

Alfred Tuke, with his bristling moustache and dignified presence, had overseen the launch and early days of this great project, but on 30th October 1907, he died. For his employers, it was a devastating blow. All agreed that he would be a hard act to follow, but it was decreed that nothing must interrupt the smooth running of the great establishment he had created. He would have wanted it that way.

Within days, Alfred Tuke's place was taken by James Brown who held the post until April 1912, when Alfred Morris was transferred from Liverpool to succeed him. It was a smooth change-over made possible by the outstanding quality of the staff employed.

For example, Henry Plesch, the head porter in 1909, was noted for speaking eight languages fluently, and international visitors were already beating a path to his door. Among the first foreign VIPs to

Princes Street in 1905

The splendid main staircase in 1914

Louis XIV drawing room in 1914, later the Pompadour Restaurant.

A sparkling example of a Caledonian Railway engine on exhibition in 1958. It was boasted by the owners that you could see your reflection in the engine surface.

be entertained that year was a high powered delegation from the Russian Government, then known as the third Duma. It had been set up by Tsar Nicholas II and was led by its president, Mr Honyakoff, and included Count Bobinsky, a former student of Edinburgh University. Russia was still recovering from its defeat by Japan in 1905 and the party was touring the UK in the hope of negotiating a substantial bank loan.

High rates did not appear to put anybody off. In an increasingly mobile world, guests were reassured that letters and telegrams would be delivered immediately upon their receipt to Private Sitting Rooms. Visitors who occupied bedrooms only were asked to apply to Reception where letters and telegrams would be kept until asked for, a notice being left in the bedroom to advise guests who might have gone out for the day.

When, in those days of steam trains, the boilers supplying the hotel's hot water had to be shut down during a refurbishment, it looked as if the Caley would be without hot water indefinitely. Unthinkable! Then someone had the bright idea of harnessing a spare steam locomotive and its boiler to the hotel supply system. It worked, and the guests were none the wiser.

Affluent Edinburgh residents, too, made regular use of the facilities. One such was Sir George Paul, senior partner in the old established law firm of Dundas & Wilson. In the summers immediately before 1914, the recently widowed Sir George would move from his town house in Eglinton Crescent to take up residence at his country cottage in Colinton, a distance of 10 miles from the town centre. As winter approached, he would move back into town again, and on both occasions, while his staff were sent on ahead to make things ready for him, he would book into the Caledonian Hotel for a week.

The First World War changed many things. After hostilities were announced on 4 August 1914, many of the Caledonian's members of staff left for military service, never to return. In the meantime, the hotel remained open despite supplies being rationed. A spirit of survival prevailed among the population, not least when in 1916, a zeppelin raid took place and bombs were dropped within 100 yards of the hotel, shattering some of the windows.

Sandy James, who had been the Caledonian's doorman since shortly before it had opened, was called up. When the war was over, he returned to his post with four wound stripes on his left sleeve, all – according to his daughter– acquired through the accidental discharge of his own rifle! Sandy was to become an institution at the Caley, remaining resplendent in his braided commissionaire's uniform for the ensuing 20 years.

My dearest Sete . . .
The hotel was warned about 8pm and everybody had a look of expectancy, but very calm nevertheless. One of our waiters was killed at his home up near Nicholson Square, and of course there were other casualties. We are on the look out every night now as they are sure to make another attempt, but no doubt we shall be able to cope with them.

A good many people went to the cellar, but Mrs Corrie and I took one whiff and our delicate organs of smell could not stand the fumes of hot humanity, so we stayed on the ground floor instead. We thought if we were going to be bombed we would like a space, anyway. One man came down in a top hat and pyjamas - a funny looking sight! We didn't go to bed until 2.30.

It really wasn't so bad after all - however, I kept a candle and matches by my bedside, also my best pyjamas and frillies, etc . . . 'cause if we are going to Kingdom Come we may as well be presentable!

An extract from a contemporary letter written by a hotel guest to a friend in Torquay, postmarked 10.30pm on 7 April 1916, gives a typically British account of what took place.

Sandy was a big man with a ginger moustache, and he knew everybody. He was born in Nairn in the north of Scotland and began work in a Perth hotel, arriving at the Princes Street Station Hotel shortly before the opening. He and his family lived at Gorgie, a short distance from his work, and each day he would take a two hour break and return home for lunch, still dressed in his stiff-fronted white shirt, black bow tie and dark blue, gold braided uniform. He considered it part of his job to know the train timetables by heart and would provide the necessary details to anybody who asked, working with cab drivers from John Croall & Sons who were located in a small office at the station entrance. There were also the car rental agencies he called 'The Daimler Boys', garages which

Managing The 'Caley'

Mr Alfred Tuke 1903–1907

Mr James Brown 1907–1912

Mr Alfred Morris 1912–1934

Mr Nicol 1934

Mr August 1940

Mr Gross 1942

Mr Findland

Mr Reg Turnbull 1948–1950

Mr Addi Jibb 1950–1960

Mr Moulin 1960

Mr Jimmy Ballantine

Mr Raymond McQuire

Mr Bill Currie

Mr John Whittingham

Mr Donald McLeod 1976–1982

Mr Alan Deeson 1982–1984

Mr Alan Blest 1984–1985

Mr Dermot Fitzpatrick 1985–1990

Mr David Clarke 1990–1994

Mr Steven Carter 1994–1998

Mr Enda Mullin 1998–2000

Ms Dagmar Mühle 2000-Present

Sandy James

hired out smart vehicles to guests who wanted to make excursions into the surrounding countryside.

Sandy was so popular at the Caley that his daughters thought he must own the place. During the Abdication Crisis of 1937, an American journalist asked him what the British man and woman in the street thought of Mrs Wallis Simpson's relationship with King Edward VIII, and much to his embarrassment, he found himself quoted on the subject in both the Washington and New York newspapers. There was also a printed recommendation that anybody who wanted a reliable summary of public opinion in the United Kingdom should immediately contact the doorman of the Caledonian Hotel in Edinburgh, Scotland.

Sandy reluctantly retired shortly before the outbreak of the Second World War. He died a few weeks later, only thirteen days after the death of his wife, to whom he had been devoted.

GOD BLESS
OUR KING
AND QUEEN

ROYAL TRIBUTE

The Caledonian pays tribute to King George V and Queen Mary (above in their carriage in front of the Caledonian gates). Although Queen Victoria and her son Edward VII had tended to ignore the Scottish palace of Holyroodhouse, things changed after George V's coronation in 1911. With an awareness of the importance of Scotland in her husband's lineage, it did not take long for Queen Mary to begin improvements on the interiors of their official Scottish home. Thereafter, Royal visits to Edinburgh and the attendant garden parties became more frequent. And the Royal Household in Scotland has retained its old traditions to this day.

Hotel with a view

The view into Queensferry Street in 1907.

1918–1945

Pompadour and Goldfish

In 1918, in the aftermath of the war, Great Britain was designated by David Lloyd George, the outgoing prime minister, 'a land fit for heroes to live in.' It was the old order that was now under attack.

Soldiers who had risked their lives for king and country now demanded a better deal both socially and in the work place. With the first Labour Government being elected to power in 1922, business interests, in particular, took steps to ensure their survival. In 1923, the Caledonian Railway Company merged with its old ally, the larger London, Midland and Scottish Railway, which by then had become the largest hotel operating company in Europe.

There also came about a major re-think on how railways were operated and, in particular, the way in which customers were looked after once they had reached their destinations. Overseeing the Caledonian Railway Company take-over on behalf of London, Midland and Scottish was Arthur Towle, son of Sir William Towle, who had been responsible for master-minding the creation of many of the great British hotels of the 19th century. Arthur Towle could therefore draw upon a wealth of past experience, and one of his first initiatives at the Caledonian Station Hotel in Edinburgh was to publish

Hotel with a view

Princes Street (ca. 1920)

TARIFF AND CHARGES

APARTMENTS

		PER DAY
Single Bed-rooms - - - - - -	from	8s. 6d.
Double Bed-rooms, Large Bed (Occupied by One Person), - - - -	from	10s. 6d.
Double Bed-rooms (Occupied by Two Persons), - - - - -	from	15s. 0d.
Double-Bedded Rooms - - - - -	from	16s. 0d.
Double Bed-rooms (with Private Bath-room), - - - - - - -	from	25s. 0d.
Double-Bedded Rooms (with Bath) -	from	30s. 0d.
Sitting-rooms, - - - - - -	from	17s. 6d.
Sitting-room, Double Bed-room with Private Bath-Room, *en suite*, - -	from	42s. 0d.
Drawing-room, Dining-room, two Double-Bedded Rooms, one Double Room, two Private Bath-rooms, and W.C., all in Private Corridor, - - -		84s. 0d.

Numerous smaller suites at proportionate charges
These prices include attendance and lights

Visitors' Servant's Bed-room, - -	from	4s. 6d.
Board, - - - - - - - -	from	7s. 6d.
Baths—Sponge Bath in Bed-room, -		1s. 0d.
Hot or Cold Bath in Bath-room,		1s. 6d.

Fires—Day, 3s. Evening, 2s.

The Tariff for Rooms and Meals is subject to revision during the busy Season—June, July, August and September.

11

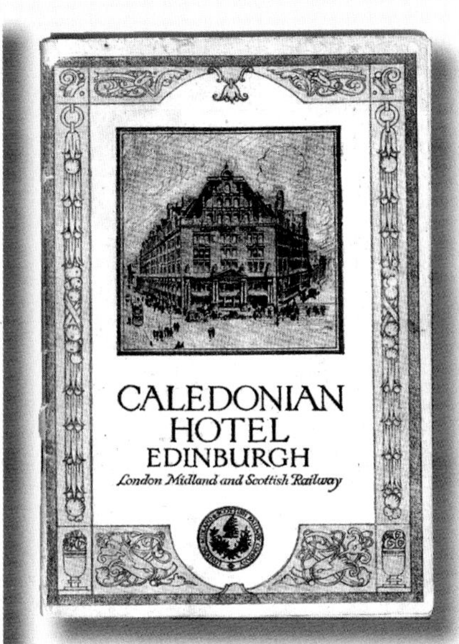

The 1920s booklet

MEALS

BREAKFAST	
Tea, Coffee, or Chocolate, with Preserves, - - - -	2s. 6d.
Table d'Hote Breakfast, from 8 a.m. till 10 a.m., as per Daily Menu, - - - -	4s. 0d.
LUNCHEON	
Table d'Hote Luncheon, from 12.30 to 2.30 p.m., as per Daily Menu, - - - -	4s 6d.
DINNER	
Table d'Hote Dinner, from 6.30 to 8.30 p.m., as per Daily Menu, Service *a la carte*	7s. 6d.
TEA, etc.	
Tea, Coffee or Chocolate, per cup,	0s. 6d.
Afternoon Tea (served in Lounge),	1s. 6d.
Tea, Coffee, or Chocolate with Honey, Marmalade or Jam, -	2s. 6d.

There is a complete Telephone Exchange in Entrance Hall connecting with all Private Sitting-rooms, on which local and trunk messages may be passed.

All Meals taken in Private Apartments are charged *a la carte* prices.

For a lengthened stay during the Winter months arrangements may be made at special inclusive rates.

Dogs are not allowed in any of the Public Rooms of the Hotel.

12

Just think about it. A coal fire was an extra 3s and baths – sponge in bedroom or hot and cold in bathroom – were charged separately, too.

For a lengthened stay during Winter months arrangements may be made at special inclusive rates.

a promotional booklet. Incorporating twenty-three pages of local advertising, it must easily have covered the printing costs and might even have made the hotel a small profit!

An excerpt from the booklet tells us that:

'There are, within the Hotel, two hundred and fifty bedrooms and seventy bathrooms, besides spacious public rooms and conveniences of every kind and the accommodation is varied enough to meet all wishes. The accommodation ranges from the Royal suite of apartments, in which Majesty itself may find a home, and family suites, which may be shut off in their subsidiary corridors from the rest of the house, to the single and double bedrooms of more ordinary demand. On whatever floor visitors may choose their rooms, and whatever scale they may elect to live, they are assured of the most exceptional quarters and the most perfect attendance and cuisine.

'Every contrivance which modern ingenuity has devised for the comfort and convenience of guests has been adopted in the house. All possibility of dust, noise and draughts is excluded by the use of turnstile doors and double and private sitting rooms by the fact that these are approached by subsidiary corridors shut off by doors from the main passages of the Hotel. At the same time, a pleasant temperature is maintained throughout the whole house by an ingenious arrangement of the calorifiers, which send heated water to every floor, and the exhausted air of the building is drawn off, noiselessly and unperceived, by revolving fans. In every public room, the promptest attendance is assured by a service system of pneumatic tubes: and by means of lifts, direct from the kitchen to every floor, meals can be served in any private apartment with the utmost celerity and 'piping hot.'

To provide a fuller picture of what the Caley's ground floor accommodation was like at this time, the brochure continues: 'The entrance hall, within its Vankannal doors, is wainscoted with mahogany and, besides the lifts for passengers and luggage,

Close-ups

MADAME POMPADOUR

No expense was spared and within two years (1923–1925) the Pompadour restaurant was created within the former entrance arches. In homage to the haute cuisine which would make it world famous, it took the name of Louis XV's formidable mistress Madame de Pompadour. Right: Chef de Cuisine Paul Newman now oversees all the hotel's kitchens.

contains the reception and bill offices, telephone exchanges, and entrance to the hairdresser's saloon. Out of the main hall, beyond, opens the spacious lounge – a pleasant resort for gossip over tea-cups of an afternoon, or the post-prandial cigar. It forms the ante-chamber for the great Georgian dining room. This fine apartment, eighty-one feet long, thirty-one broad and twenty-six high, is pillared <sic> and wainscoted with mahogany and with its gilded spindrels and great carved mantelpieces, its green morocco chairs and rich red carpet, rivals any baronial hall of olden times.'

As splendid as the great ground floor Georgian dining room may have been in 1923, Arthur Towle had other ideas. Within two years he had transformed the sixty foot long by twenty foot broad Louis XIV drawing room on the first floor into the much celebrated Pompadour Restaurant. With large windows overlooking the gardens of Edinburgh's West End, this was an ideal, intimate space to cater for a limited number of guests.

No expense was spared. The building work cost £1,500 with an additional £1,500 for new furniture and £1,160 for crockery and linen. The walls of the restaurant were covered in gold brocade, and in homage to the *haute cuisine* which would make it world famous, it took the name of Louis XV's formidable mistress Madame de Pompadour, who lived from 1721 to 1764, and for twenty years virtually governed France.

There was a dinner dance every evening, featuring dinners with as many as 12 courses: *hors d'oeuvre*, soup, egg dish, fish, *entrée*, grill, roast, dessert, savoury, cold buffet, fruit and cheese. The Pompadour soon became the most fashionable eating place in town, retaining its status well into the 1930s and attracting a stylish clientele from far and wide. Among those who made discreet occasional bookings for dinner were the Prince of Wales, later Edward VIII and Duke of Windsor, accompanied by his brother, the Duke of Kent, who would afterwards embark upon a visit to the Fountain-

Hotel with a view

Opposite the hotel was a department store owned by Robert Maul and Son. The corner was soon nicknamed 'Maule's Corner'. Robert Easton Stuart painted 'Maule's Corner After The Rain' in 1925 (oil on canvas). The iron gate in the foreground belongs to the Caledonian Railway Station, right next to the hotel's entrance. We will meet (at) this corner again in this book and therefore it is useful to know that it later became 'Binns', then 'Frasers'.

The heir to the throne, the Prince of Wales. Sandy salutes.

bridge Palais de Dance to enjoy a night of anonymous amusement. Until recently there were still elderly ladies in the town who distinctly remembered being asked to dance by a boyish young toff with blonde hair who bore a striking resemblance to the heir to the throne. Imagine what the tabloid press would make of such Royal exploits nowadays!

Scotland's capital was keeping pace with the times. Horse drawn trams were replaced with the electric variety, with tram lines plumbed into the street. Wealthy Scottish society travelled into town from their country estates to shop at the elegant, largely family-owned stores of Princes Street, notably Maule's Emporium, Darlings, Greensmith Downes, Melrose's Tea & Coffee Merchants, Thornton & Co, R.W. Forsyth and Jenners. Of these, only Jenners, founded in 1833 and the world's oldest independent department store, remains.

Then as now, the privacy of guests at the Caley was of paramount importance. Despite the recession of the early 1930s, under general managers Morris and Nicol, the hotel enjoyed the patronage of the elite of British, European and American society, many of them on their way to shooting and stalking house parties in the Highlands. Some even brought their entire staff with them, often kitted out in livery uniform.

In truth though, Edinburgh's reputation at this time was often austere and occasionally provincial. It encompassed the way of life so intuitively depicted in Muriel Spark's classic novel *The Prime*

'Yes, we are all proud to be working here!'
To the left, the famous Sandy. The picture was taken in 1935.

of Miss Jean Brodie, the film of which was to earn Maggie Smith the 1969 Academy Award nomination for best actress. Against this background of propriety and double standards, however, grand society balls took place under glittering chandeliers at the Caley and in the city's Assembly Rooms in George Street.

And then, once again, Britain was at war. Once again many of the staff were called up for military service and war time restrictions came into force. Unlike many other hotels throughout the country, however, the Caledonian was not requisitioned by the Government, although it was heavily patronised by the Forces, especially young American and Canadian soldiers and airmen. Memories obviously lingered, for in the decades that followed many of them returned to the hotel to holiday there with their families.

Happily, the city of Edinburgh itself remained surprisingly unscathed in those dark years. The bulk of the enemy bombing raids on Scotland targeted naval installations on the north side of the Firth of Forth, and Clydebank on the West Coast. At the Caley, diners were advised that they could enjoy a meat or fish dish, but not both, and remarkably the dining room continued to serve its own home-smoked salmon. This was prepared under the strict supervision of Chef Kung who ruled over his kitchen like an Eastern mogul, terrifying any member of staff who stepped out of line by seizing a meat cleaver and demanding that they get out of his kitchen. Understandably, nobody was prepared to divulge the source of his Tweed salmon.

A framed certificate featuring military insignia gives some indication as to the esteem in which the hotel was held by those servicemen who made use of it during those troubled times: the Canadian Knights of Columbus honoured The Caledonian Hotel, Edinburgh, in recognition of distinguished services to men and women of the Canadian Armed Forces 1939–46.

In 1946 Edinburgh, there was only one licensed restaurant that was not part of a hotel, and that closed at 10pm on weekdays. It was not open at all on Sundays. So there was no question about it, the dance floor at the de Guise was the place to go if you could afford to. Throughout the war, and afterwards, it was presided over by charismatic head waiter Mario Brenna.

One of the regulars had this to say about him:

'The decoration of the old Pomp and the de Guise had to be seen to be appreciated. Yet in spite of the lavish surroundings both were always welcoming. There was never a stuffed atmosphere, no matter the occasion. Mario saw to that. He was a genius. Always hit the right tone. Dignity personified, but friendly with it.'

The same gentleman also remembered attending a wedding reception in the de Guise: 'The menu was in French, of course, and only

In 1938, it was decided to close the Pompadour Restaurant and replace it with the de Guise Restaurant situated on the ground floor. The restaurant was named after Marie de Guise, the French mother of Mary Queen of Scots. In keeping with demand, this was accessed by an entrance from Rutland Street and featured a larger dance floor. The staff of the de Guise Restaurant poses during the 1950s, Mario in the center.

a handful of the guests had any fluency. Mario and his staff were marvellous in explaining everything. I knew one guest who took his family to France for that year just because of Mario. And he made the bride feel like the Queen of Sheba. But it was never overdone. Everything was just right, even the music for the dancing. Cam Robbie was my great favourite. Cam and Henry Hall somehow again hit just the right note!'

Such was the regard in which he was held that when Mario eventually retired, his customers clubbed together to have his portrait painted.

Geoffrey Anderson was a young officer in the Cheshire Regiment. Early on in the war, he had won a military cross for bravery. He had been captured by Italian forces in Africa and made a prisoner of war in Italy. He had then escaped, but had been recaptured and sent to Germany, from where he had been liberated. It had been a traumatic war for him, and in 1946, he was sent to convalesce in Dunbar.

In Dunbar, there was not much to do of an evening, but one night he and some friends discovered that there was a train to Edinburgh that would take them to the Saturday dinner dance at the de Guise. That same night, Anna Brock from Linlithgow had been taken to the de Guise by her three brothers as a treat. Geoffrey saw Anna across the dance floor and after some hesitation, summoned up the courage to ask her to dance. They were married a year later and, according to their daughter Caroline Pearson, talked often of that first romantic encounter on the dance floor of the de Guise.

Royal romance was also in the air. In 1947, the then Princess Elizabeth and her future husband, the young Lieutenant Philip Mountbatten, dined at the Caley with the Duke and Duchess of Buccleuch. Guests were seated at an oval, candle-lit table with a mirrored centrepiece framed in wrought silver to reflect the gleaming silver of the candle-sticks. The Duchess confided afterwards that everybody was delighted and that personally, she was unable to remember having enjoyed a better dinner, even before the war.

In the same room, three days later, Princess Elizabeth, Lieutenant Mountbatten and Princess Margaret were the guests of Field Marshal Lord Wavell, a former viceroy of India, and the officers of the Highland Brigade. This time, the guests dined at the High Sheriff Table. An illuminated playing fountain contained live gold fish in its hollow, and wrought iron stands sported flower decorations in hanging bowls. In each bowl swam two goldfish. It was a novel idea. The goldfish were borrowed from Edinburgh Zoo and were returned the following morning.

Afterwards, one of the organisers, Lieutenant David Balfour, wrote to Mr Goss, the general manager, and said that General Neil McMicking, the regiment's commanding officer, and many others who were privileged to be present, had voted it the best dinner they had ever eaten. Such praise, in those days was, in his opinion, the highest accolade that could be afforded to the Caledonian's chef and 'his worthy assistants.'

As the 1950s approached, life in Edinburgh was slowly returning to pre-war normality. After dinner one evening, 17-year old Princess Margaret departed promptly at 10pm to attend the Victoria League Ball held in the Assembly Rooms. Two nights previously she had been dancing to Tim Wright's Scottish Country Dance Band in the New Cavendish Ballroom.

Major developments were taking place throughout the city. Over the course of the next decade, the electric trams which had served the general public since the 1920s were phased out and replaced by buses. But Edinburgh's long-established nickname of 'Auld Reekie' lingered on. This originated from mediaeval times when the slops and refuse of the Old Town were simply tossed into the streets for removal. Although that practice was long gone, there remained the smoke from thousands of tenement chimneys which combined with the mist of the seasonal North Sea *ha'*, to form an all-enveloping, impenetrable smog that sometimes lasted for days and perpetuated the Auld Reekie myth. By the 1960s, however, Edinburgh had become smokeless, and on windless nights the only aroma was the pervasive and locally much-cherished aroma of malt evaporating from the breweries, mixed with just a tinge of grain whisky from the North British Distillery at Fountainbridge.

The darling of the City, Sir Sean Connery, arrives at The Caledonian.

Into Show Business

In 1947, a bold initiative was launched that would dramatically influence and entirely alter the character of Scotland's Capital – The Edinburgh Festival of Music and Drama. It was an unlikely and courageous enterprise for a traditionally Protestant city located in the north of an island off the west coast of Europe. Endorsed by Sir John Falconer, Edinburgh's Lord Provost, it has since grown into the largest artistic and cultural event of its kind in the world.

A sense of deliverance prevailed in the aftermath of the war years. Here was an opportunity to celebrate peace and heal the wounds of world conflict. It was an inspired vision. Following a series of discussions, and with the full agreement of the Corporation of the City of Edinburgh, the experiment began.

Author A J Stewart has a particularly vivid memory of that August day: 'I am standing at Binns' Corner, formerly Maule's Corner. Everyone met at Binns' Corner, because it commanded every approach to the city. The trams from Fairmilehead decanted their passengers at the stop beside the east wall of the Caledonian Hotel. The bus which came from Davidsons Mains stopped in Queensferry Street. Thus I am standing facing the Caledonian Hotel as crowds

of other people awaiting people, begin to talk to me – and to each other – and some of us (like myself) are almost crying with joy, and I say to somebody 'The War is over! The War is finally over!'

'And we are all indicating the traffic island in Shandwick Place, upon which stood a stone pedestal clock (another good reason for meeting at Binns'/Maules' Corner) which bore the Roman numerals and squiggly cast iron work of every municipal clock established since the 19th century.

'The Island, as I knew it, had been covered with black tarmac like everything else in my life since 1939. There, suddenly, the clock was surrounded by tiers of colour. Massed banks of flowers, a glorious infinity of herbaceous border, all somehow assembled by the Works Department of the City to open the first Edinburgh International Arts Festival. '

On Sunday 24 August 1947, the then Princess Elizabeth and Princess Margaret attended a concert in the Usher Hall, and for the ensuing three weeks Edinburgh revelled in its cosmopolitan celebrity. Famous names flocked from the far corners of the globe to take part, and with the subsequent introduction of five more simultaneous festivals – Fringe, Jazz, Film, Book and Television, and the Edinburgh Military Tattoo – have continued to do so ever since.

And from the start, it was the Caledonian Hotel with its established reputation for comfort, service and privacy, which provided the home base for the stars. Sir John Barbirolli, Kathleen Ferrier, Sir Malcolm Sargeant, Sir Alec Guinness, and prima ballerina Margot Fonteyn were among those who participated in the early programmes. Todd Duncan, who played Porgy in the musical *Porgy and Bess*, stayed in a suite. In another part of the hotel, Sir Laurence Olivier paced the floor while a member of the secretarial staff made changes to his script.

Thereafter, Edinburgh became used to welcoming the great entertainers of the age. It would be impossible to include a full list of

Pets Welcome

When Hollywood cowboy Roy Rogers appeared with his wife Dale Evans at the Empire Theatre on 1 March 1954, he brought with him his famous white wonder horse Trigger, and they ascended the grand staircase together. It was reported in the newspapers that Trigger spent the night in the Versailles Suite, and photographs were taken of a bed of hay that had been made up for him, and his hair brush that had been placed on a dressing table. In actual fact, Trigger was smuggled out in the early hours of the morning to bed down with his double called Tarzan in the nearby stables of the St Cuthbert's Co-operative Society. Nonetheless, it was a superb publicity stunt.

Who's Who

Who's Who

Stan Laurel and Oliver Hardy – 'carried in' by a Caledonian porter.

those in town for the year long calendar of official functions, or those playing at the city's theatres: the King's, Royal Lyceum, Playhouse, and more recently, the Edinburgh Festival Theatre. However, Judy Garland was one of the first big names to visit after the war. Then came Charlie Chaplin, Jeanette MacDonald, Charles Boyer, Ginger Rogers, Marlon Brando, Bette Davis, Fred McMurray, Dame Anna Neagle, Diana Dors and James Robertson Justice.

Stewart Scoular, later room services manager, began working as a waiter in the de Guise Restaurant in 1951 at the age of 15, but his age meant that he was obliged to return home from the hotel at 10pm. One night he discovered that there was to be a private function for Noel Coward, and he was devastated when told he was too young to be in attendance.

In April 1953, Gene Kelly arrived with his producer Arthur Freed, and the lyricist of *Singing in the Rain*, and the great song and dance man could not resist performing a few impromptu steps up and down the grand staircase.

There was further excitement when comedians Stan Laurel and Oliver Hardy visited on 13 April. The story goes that Stan accidentally spilled his coffee onto one of the hotel's crisp white table cloths and Ollie, quick as a flash, turned to the waiter with a wink and uttered his famous catchphrase: 'Now look what a fine mess you've got me into Stanley.'

Hollywood just could not stay away. In June 1953, America's sweetheart Mary Pickford arrived with her husband Buddy Rogers. Anne Ziegler and Webster Booth, Cliff Richards, George Chisholm, Charles Aznavour, Count Basie, Oscar Peterson, Johnny Dankworth, Tom Jones, Stephane Grapelli, Annie Lennox, The Everley Brothers, Humphrey Lyttleton, Andy Williams, Shirley Bassey, Roy Orbison, Eartha Kitt, Norman Vaughan and David Bowie are among the many singers and musicians who have patronised the Caley over the second half of the last century. In 1958, singer Mario Lanza was photographed enjoying a gargantuan meal in the de

Guise, and later that same year, the legendary Paul Robeson, star of *Show Boat*, checked in.

Also during the 1950s, the 'cry' singer Johnny Ray brought traffic in the street outside to a standstill when his fans invaded the hotel foyer, and a young Tommy Steele turned up with his arm in a sling, having been mobbed by fans in Dundee. Stewart Scoular (now somewhat older than when we first met him), whose career at the Caley spanned forty years, told of a night when Billy Daniels, Annie Ross and Tessy O'Shea were in residence. Gathered together in the bar, Billy turned to the staff and said: 'You guys have looked after us. Now we'd like to entertain you.' And the three stars grouped around the piano to sing 'That Old Black Magic'.

Bob Hope and Bing Crosby stayed at the hotel in the days before refrigerators were an essential catering accessory, and Crosby insisted that one be provided for his room. During one visit, Hope could not resist playing the clown and there were reports of him sitting in a corner of the Caley lounge wearing a dunce's cap.

Concierge Billy Garioch, who started with the hotel as a page boy in the 1950s and then became a porter and barman in the old American Bar (later the Boardroom), self-deprecatingly recalls being asked by Crosby's wife to bring up the couple's bags from the car. To his dismay, he found the luggage included not only a suitcase, but a heavy set of exercise weights as well. A small man, it took him a good half an hour to struggle upstairs to their suite with the luggage and weights. When he arrived, gasping for breath, Mrs Crosby said: 'Oh, I'm sorry. I didn't mean you should take the weights.' She was kind enough, he said, not to ask him to take them back.

Harry Klar, who began work as a porter in 1946, was taken to the cinema by The Shadows when they came to Edinburgh to perform and stay at the Caley during the 1950s. 'We were all about the same age, and they just invited me to join them,' he explained. 'It was a great laugh. You never knew who you were going to meet in this job.' For example, in April 1970, he and Jimmy Reilly, also a porter,

Who's Who

Who's Who

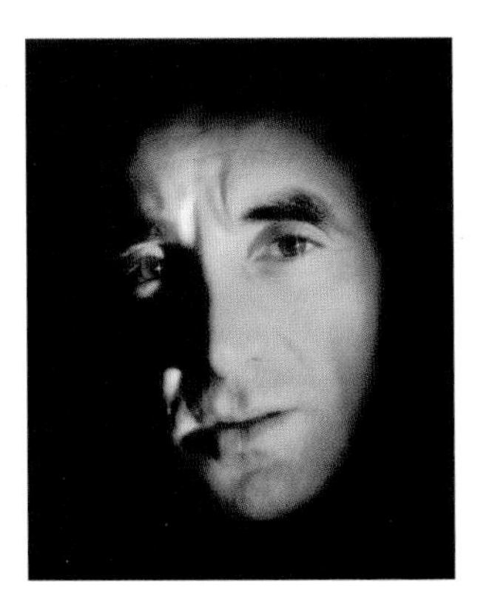

Left page: Sir Charles Chaplin signed in, Fred MacMurray and wife enjoyed the hotel, Perry Como performed at the Royal Lyceum Theatre, singer Mario Lanza enjoyed the de Guise restaurant, Bing Crosby insisted that a refrigerator was provided for his room, Bette Davis brought more Hollywood splendour to the 'Caley' and so did David Niven.

Right page: Richard Burton and Elizabeth Taylor took a break from filming 'The Taming of the Shrew', the great voices of Shirley Bassey and Charles Aznavour echoed through the hallways of the hotel.

escorted the Queen Mother to the wrong floor in the lift when she came to the Caley to attend a lunch in the Montrose Room organised by Midlothian County Council. 'That's alright,' she told them graciously. 'That sort of thing is always happening to me.'

For the 1957 Festival, the great diva Maria Callas was on stage at the King's Theatre with La Piccola Scala Milan, and journalist Ian Crawford, later the festival's press officer, was granted an interview with her in her room. Crawford recalls her being both surprisingly slight and taller than he had expected, but there were those famous large eyes and the expressively sensual mouth. Her husband, Giovanni Battista Meneghini, a small, square man who bore a passing resemblance to the Italian dictator Mussolini, lay on the bed and made disparaging remarks in Italian until she rounded upon him and told him to leave the room.

Thereafter, the interview progressed fluently until the end when Crawford asked her if she would like to hear the recording. He rewound the tape and turned the recorder on. There was a distant rumble of traffic, but nothing else. 'What do we do now?' asked Callas.

Knowing that she had the reputation for eating journalists for breakfast, Crawford tried to make light of it. 'Be a tempestuous diva and throw me and my box of tricks out of the window,' he said.

Fortunately, she laughed. 'Send for another machine and I will do it again,' she announced imperiously.

In 1963, Roddy Martine, co-author of this book, was a schoolboy editing a teenage Edinburgh Festival magazine called *Lens*. Much to his delight, he was granted an interview with violinist Sir Yehudi Menuhin, and when he knocked on the door of the hotel suite and was told to enter, he found the great man standing on his head in the midst of his customary yoga routine. Also present in the room was Menuhin's sister Hephizibah, who was playing the piano;

Yehudi Menuhin, interviewed at the hotel by Roddy Martine in 1963. Menuhins' son had been born while he and his wife were staying there during the first festival of 1947.

she broke off from doing so to pour coffee. Menuhin subsequently revealed that he had a special affection for the Caledonian Hotel because their son had been born while he and his wife were staying there during the first festival of 1947.

Marlene Dietrich came to the Caley for the festivals of 1963 and 1964 to perform late night cabaret at the Royal Lyceum Theatre. She requested a king size bed for her room, and Jack Herkes, who had started as a joiner in the hotel in 1960, was given the task of building it. The bed was later adapted for the 6ft 4in frame of Clint Eastwood when he came to stay. Extra-long beds were also requested for the Harlem Globetrotters, and Jack remembered hearing

Marlene Dietrich

about the double bed provided for Queen Salote of Tonga, 'the tallest Queen of the world's smallest Kingdom,' when she visited Scotland following the Coronation of Queen Elizabeth in 1953. 'They had to reinforce it from below,' he recalled.

Although she had a reputation for being difficult, Marlene Dietrich was a consummate professional when it came to her adoring public. Autograph seekers were never turned away, and she would leave little gifts for the members of the hotel staff whom she felt had looked after her particularly well.

Having bankrolled a controversial breakaway Oxford Group, Four Degrees Under, in the 1966 Fringe, Richard Burton and Elizabeth Taylor took a break from filming *The Taming of the Shrew* in Mantua with Franco Zeffirelli. The play was considered 'progressive' with lines such as 'God is fab. God is here.' At the time, Burton and Taylor were the golden superstar couple, but thanks to the discretion of the Caley, they managed to keep their Edinburgh sojourn relatively low profile. In fact, it was so low profile that when they arrived, not even the deputy manager recognised them. Noticing them sitting in the lobby while their room was being prepared, he was about to comment on Burton's scruffy jeans and open neck shirt, when Elizabeth Taylor looked up and he recognised her. They had just arrived from the airport and afterwards dressed up to the occasion.

John Gibson, veteran columnist with the *Edinburgh Evening News*, vividly recalls a one-to-one meeting with screen siren Sophia Loren

Personal service at the Caledonian Hotel: Actress Joan Collins is waited upon by well-known Edinburgh Evening News columnist John Gibson.

in her suite. Years later, he was still talking about the silky rustle of her stockings as she crossed her elegant legs. On another occasion he was present when American singer Guy Mitchell, in Edinburgh to play at the Empire Theatre, attempted to have a barbecue in his room. 'There were about a dozen of us present,' said Gibson. 'Guy was wearing a stetson hat and was flushed with the success of his latest hit song 'She Wore Red Feathers.' He decided he was going to give us a full red-blooded Texas cook-in and lit a fire in the fireplace. But what he did not know was that the chimney was blocked. It was a fun idea, but the room filled up with smoke and the fire brigade had to be called.'

One evening, the Caley's resident pianist Pete Seaton, a well-known local musician, was playing in the lounge when he was requested by singer Mel Torme to accompany him while he sang a couple of songs. The New Seekers came to stay in March 1972 to represent Great Britain in the Eurovision Song Contest held at the Usher Hall that year, and once again the fans were out in force outside of the Caley's main entrance, hoping to catch a glimpse of their idols.

Elton John was a regular guest when on his various tours, and he always insisted that his suite be filled with white lilies and bottles of diet cola. Famously not wishing to draw attention to himself, he would arrive wearing dark glasses and an enormous stetson hat, and once signed himself 'Donald Schwartzkopf.'

Lou Reed, also in search of privacy, called room service to ask for a video recorder to be delivered to his room. When told that this would take 20 minutes, he asked delivery to be postponed for an hour and a half, as he would be busy with his daily meditation routine during that time.

Another big star who has regularly made the Caley his home is Sir Sean Connery. He was born in a simple tenement house less than a mile away at Fountainbridge, so it is all the more understandable that the Caley should become a firm favourite of his. One senior member of staff, who had hitherto not counted herself an admirer, encountered

The 1960s brought us a former chorus boy, body builder and model chosen by a Daily Express readers' poll to play the role of Ian Fleming's superspy, James Bond: his name was Sean Connery. Two years before his death in 1964, Fleming saw his hero on screen for the first time, hunting the evil Dr No.

Sir Sean – he has since been knighted – is a regular at the 'Caley' and Edinburgh's local hero. The staff is always proud to pose with him. So were former resident manager Peter Hales and former general manager Enda Mullin.

him one day in the hotel shop buying a newspaper. 'It was so wonderful, the way he said Good Morning,' she breathed afterwards. 'I just melted!'

When Clint Eastwood stayed at the hotel, he was offered a selection of 100 different beers to choose from. And speaking of beers, in 1976, Her Serene Highness Princess Grace of Monaco (making her first public appearance on the public circuit since she had married Prince Ranier and ceased being film star Grace Kelly) came to read poetry at St Cecilia's Hall at Festival. Calling for room service, she surprisingly asked for lager, whereupon Stewart Scoular suggested she try pale ale instead. Afterwards, she coyly admitted that she had rather enjoyed it.

'Of course, our whole training is based upon non-personal involvement with guests,' observed a member of staff at the time. 'But Princess Grace was so beautiful and so regal and so pleasant with it that we could hardly keep our eyes off her. I can tell you, all our training and discipline was sorely put to the test. She had this wonderful dignity, and I swear she looked even more stunning in person than on screen, and I have seen all of her films. I think the whole hotel, staff as well as guests, were in awe of her great beauty – and perhaps just a little bit in love.'

After Princess Grace, Stewart Scoular's favourite guest was undoubtedly Peter Ustinov, who came to Edinburgh to produce *Don Giovani* at the 1974 Festival, and *The Marriage* in 1982. 'A real gentleman,' said Stewart. 'You met everybody when you did room service. It was a great opportunity to find out what people were really like. Some were wonderful and others were not, but you always respected their privacy.'

Today, every available nook and cranny of the city is co-opted as a Fringe Festival venue during the month of August. And for some time during the late 1970s, the left luggage room at the Caley was used as a theatre space: among acts that appeared there were a

Ballet star Rudolph Nureyev (top: with Roddy Martine, below with Festival Director Frank Dunlop) often came to Edinburgh to perform, first with the Royal Ballet and Scottish Ballet, and in 1984 and 1985 as the choreographer of the Paris Opera Ballet, appearing at the Playhouse Theatre. Dressed in his high boots, leather trousers and leather cap, he was a familiar figure in the hotel foyer, and on more than one occasion became so engrossed in a conversation with somebody he had met at the hotel that his audiences were kept waiting.

Berkoff play, a revue penned by the script team of *Not The Nine O'Clock News,* and the Scottish Festival Puppets.

In 1981, with the hotel under new ownership, there was some debate as to whether this practice should be allowed to continue, but after heated negotiation, the go-ahead was given for a French play, staged by the Almeida Theatre of London, and backed by the French Government. The rent for the room was £500 for a 5-week run.

Who's Who

Fiona Fullerton with resident manager Lynn Abernethy, Elton John arrived in dark glasses and a stetson hat, Billy Connolly, Anthony Quinn and William 'Count' Basie.

Dynasty star Linda Evans came to Edinburgh to attend a charity gala at the Playhouse Theatre in 1985. One day, Twiggy, arguably the world's first supermodel, came out of the hotel in a hurry. Doorman Charlie opened a cab door, doffed his hat, and said: 'Good morning! Taxi? Jenners?'

'No.' Twiggy retorted, quick as a flash. 'Walking! Marks and Spencer!'

When Catherine Zeta Jones and Michael Douglas attended the premier of Zeta Jones's film *Entrapment* at the Edinburgh Film Festival in 1999, both made full use of the hotel's leisure and beauty therapy services. The Welsh actress was sufficiently impressed with the massage she received from the resident masseuse, that she afterwards wrote to thank her personally saying that she looked forward to another session on her next visit.

The turn of the millennium brought a flood of celebrity names to the Caley for a variety of reasons. Broadcaster Gloria Hunniford stayed there for a family wedding; super chef Michel Roux, singer Kiki Dee, comedian Tim Brooke-Taylor, TV presenter Louis Theroux, television pundit Clive James, and impresario Victor Spinetti are among those who signed the visitor's book. When Shakin Stevens performed at a private function in the Castle Suite in December 2000, the chandeliers had to be load-tested beforehand to make sure that they would withstand the noise level without falling.

Stephanie Powers stayed at the hotel in April 2002, to star as English governess Anna Leonowens in the Rogers & Hammerstein stage musical of *The King and I* at the Playhouse Theatre. Among other celebrity names that year was BBC television's East Enders tough guy Martin Kemp.

Princess Anne, the Princess Royal, with general manager Dagmar Mühle and William Sleigh, President of the Edinburgh chapter of the Royal Warrant Holders.

Right: the Princess, accompanied by former general manager Dermot Fitzpatrick.

RAIL ROYALTY ROMANCE

As Edinburgh's top hotel, the Caledonian has for a century played host to Royalty, numerous presidents, prime ministers and diplomats. On more than one occasion, Indian maharajas have taken over an entire floor to accommodate their entourage. Some retired members of the Caley staff still talk of seeing the bodyguards who slept in the corridors with their knives drawn to fend off potential assassins. When US President Harry S. Truman visited, he brought with him his G-men for protection, and when one of them spotted an object on the floor, everybody was told to 'Freeze!' It turned out to be a false alarm.

Foreign Royalty, too, enjoyed the hotel's hospitality. Catherine Moir, head receptionist until she left to get married in 1955, remembers the visit of Prince Chula of Siam. 'He had a bulldog which was brought into the hall and tied to a radiator while the porters kept an eye on it. I felt so sorry for the poor creature that when I came off duty late at night I would secretly walk it around nearby Charlotte Square at midnight.'

In 1960, the King and Queen of Nepal paid a State Visit with an entourage of 20. An instruction had arrived from the Govern-

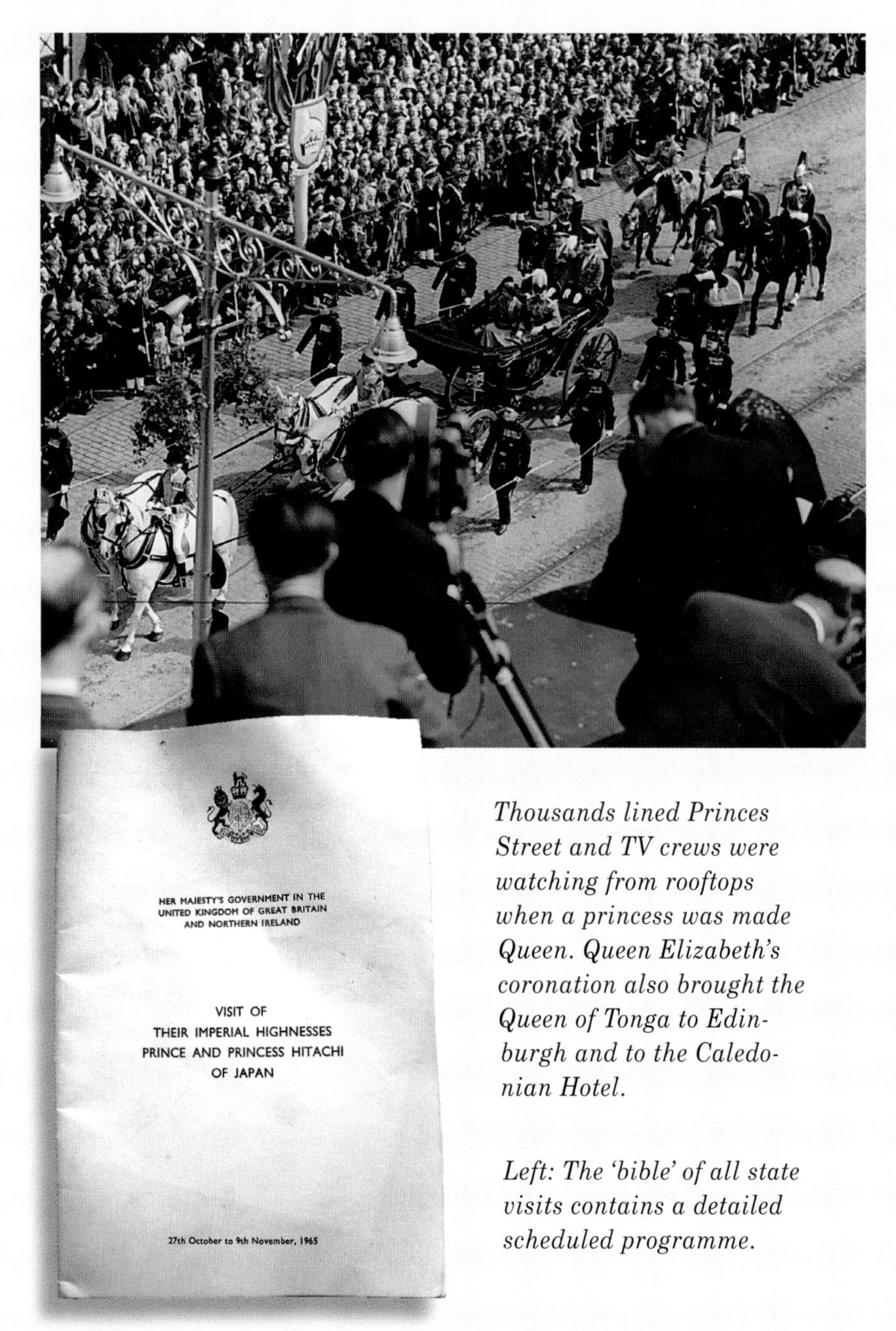

HER MAJESTY'S GOVERNMENT IN THE
UNITED KINGDOM OF GREAT BRITAIN
AND NORTHERN IRELAND

VISIT OF
THEIR IMPERIAL HIGHNESSES
PRINCE AND PRINCESS HITACHI
OF JAPAN

27th October to 9th November, 1965

Thousands lined Princes Street and TV crews were watching from rooftops when a princess was made Queen. Queen Elizabeth's coronation also brought the Queen of Tonga to Edinburgh and to the Caledonian Hotel.

Left: The 'bible' of all state visits contains a detailed scheduled programme.

King Hussein with general manager Dermot Fitzpatrick during the 1980s. King Hussein became a regular visitor to Edinburgh and the Caledonian Hotel.

Prior to his arrival, a 17- page portfolio of information on the Hashemite kingdom of Jordan was circulated to all staff.

All concerned were briefed upon the correct form of address. Ten cars were made available, checked and cleaned, including the King's Rolls Royce. Each had to fly the correct pennant.

'All managers on duty when the party arrives, two on duty each breakfast period to check each order and go in with each suite breakfast; flowers in all rooms, every member of the party to be conducted to rooms by a manager; advise switchboard of special attention to the whole party, including speeding calls to and from Jordan; fresh fruit in all rooms, fresh stock of beverages in all rooms to include ice and mineral waters and Coca Cola; breakfasts to be served on table in Royal Suite, on trolleys in bedrooms (make sure there is an ample supply of fresh orange available); crockery and cutlery to be specially set aside for 136; Newspapers (The Scotsman, The Times, The Guardian, Daily Express, Time Magazine, Newsweek, Scottish Field) in each room. Linkman on duty for each arrival and departure.'

Left: an excerpt from the portfolio

Eric Milligan, the Convenor of Lothian Region, thanks Mikhail Gorbachev, who was in Edinburgh with his wife Raisa to deliver the prestigious Lothian Lecture.

ment Hospitality Fund in London, enclosing a Nepalese flag. A red carpet was to be delivered to the station not later than 4.30 pm, together with the necessary brushes, presumably for sweeping it.

During their stay, the hotel was called upon to loan its table china for the State Dinner held for Their Majesties at Edinburgh Castle. The dinner was a great success, but Addi Jibb, The Caley's general manager, received a reprimand from his employers, British Transport Hotels: 'It is not advisable to loan our crockery on such occasions, as our name is thereby connected with the service and type of food provided – and this may be damaging to our reputation.'

In 1962, Her Imperial Highness Princess Chichibu of Japan came to the hotel on a private visit. She must have had an enjoyable stay, as she encouraged Their Imperial Highnesses Prince and Princess Hitachi of Japan to stay at the hotel as well. They did, three years later, for two weeks. Accompanying them were their Comptroller of the Household and the Vice-Grand Master of Ceremonies to His Majesty the Emperor of Japan

On an equally high profile level, in 1962 King Olav of Norway came to Scotland on a State Visit, where he was met at Princes Street Station by Her Majesty the Queen. Flags, flown from seven new flag poles on the hotel façade, were specially sent from Liverpool, and two of the hotel's linen cupboards were used by BBC engineers sent to cover the event.

When the Caley was called upon to provide the catering for the Royal Command Performance in the Royal Lyceum Theatre in Grindlay Street, next to the Usher Hall, the headquarters of British Transport Hotels was called upon to supply 42 pairs of white cotton gloves (assorted sizes) for the waiters.

In July 1966, His Majesty King Hussein I of Jordan and Her Royal Highness Princess Muna arrived at the hotel with an entourage of 25. This was another of those occasions when the Caley's reputation was put to the test in no uncertain terms. No request was too much for the staff, determined to live up to the highest standards.

Other high profile visits demanded an equal level of forward planning. For example, His Excellency Mr Wang Chen came to stay when he was vice premier of the People's Republic of China. Equally, when Pat Nixon, wife of former US President Richard Nixon came to the hotel on holiday incognito with her two daughters, discretion was the order of the day. The press only came to hear of it afterwards, and then only because it was discovered that a Mrs Louise Johnson had registered to stay at the same time. To start off with, it was assumed that this was Mrs Lyndon B Johnson, wife of the incumbent president, but there was, in fact, no connection.

Revenue manager Sarah Callaghan recalls the time when Mikhail Gorbachev was a guest in 1984. He was on his way into a luncheon being held in the ballroom, when an aide rushed up to tell him that Yuri Andropov, the then Soviet leader, had suddenly died. Sarah saw Gorbachev's face freeze. His welcoming smile completely disappeared, and he said, 'Sorry, but I have to go back.' He returned

Prince Naruhito of Japan with Lynn Abernethy – in search for the 'family man'.

The staff took Japanese lessons for their Royal visitor.

later that day to Moscow to be elected General Secretary of the Communist Party of the Soviet Union.

Gorbachev stood down as Russian President in 1991, and two years later was back in Edinburgh once again with his wife Raisa, this time to deliver the prestigious Lothian Lecture. His speech was well received, and a dinner was held at the Caley in his honour, hosted by Eric Milligan, then Convenor of Lothian Region. 'It was a momentous occasion,' he said. 'Especially as the pulling down of the Berlin Wall in 1989 was still fresh in all our minds.'

In 1991, His Imperial Highness Prince Naruhito of Japan arrived in Edinburgh during an eight day visit to the UK as patron of the Japanese Festival. Stewart Scoular had brought breakfast to his

Prime minister John Major with general manager David Clarke and resident manager Lynn Abernethy.

room. The prince looked closely at him and said, 'I believe you are the *family man.*' Stewart was baffled until the prince explained that he knew that ten years before at the Caledonian, Steward had looked after his father, then Crown Prince Akihito, now Emperor of Japan.

British politicians have been regular guests. Harry Klar, one of the hotel's longest serving porters, was once asked to pack prime minister Edward Heath's suitcase for him. Prime minister Margaret Thatcher, and Michael Foot and Neil Kinnoch, both leaders of the British Labour Party, stayed during the early 1980s, and since then, prime ministers John Major and, of course, Tony Blair.

It should be remembered that Tony Blair was at school at Fettes College in Inverleith, so he has known the Caley from an early age. According to one news report, however, there was a problem one

Old Edinburgh hand, prime minister Tony Blair with Hilton regional vice president Scotland and Ireland Larbi Allali and general manager Dagmar Mühle.

Below: a letter sent by 10, Downing Street, on an earlier occasion.

10 DOWNING STREET
LONDON SW1A 2AA

THE PRIME MINISTER

31 August 1998

Dear Steve,

Once again the Caledonian Hotel shone like a jewel in Edinburgh. The service we all received could not have been bettered.

I realise what an enormous task it is preparing for such a visit and I would be grateful if you would thank all your staff for their efforts, with particular thanks to Jim Lindsay and Gordon Clapperton.

We both thoroughly enjoyed our stay in your delightful City.

With best wishes,

Many thanks too to Sarah, who looked after us so well.

Yours ever

Tony Blair

Steve Carter Esq

night, when transvestite comedian Lily Savage fumbled back to his room after a festival night out. The comic claimed that alarmed security men, thinking that he was rather too close to the prime minister's room, pounced on him and ruined his frock! Apparently a dry cleaning bill was subsequently sent to 10, Downing Street.

In 1992, the Caledonian Hotel was officially appointed to house the European Commission and the British Government for the summit meeting of European prime ministers. Working with British prime minister John Major, who occupied the Presidential Suite, were Chancellor of the Exchequer

Norman Lamont, and Foreign Secretary Douglas Hurd. Also in residence were the President of the European Commission Jacques Delors, prime minister Professor A. Cavaco Silva of Portugal, and Spanish prime minister Felipe M. Gonzalez, accompanied by their senior ministers, advisers and administrative staffs.

'The whole city did us proud,' wrote Douglas Hurd. So impressed was he by the level of hospitality provided by the Caley that he afterwards wrote to thank resident manager Lyn Abernethy and the staff, adding that he had asked the Foreign Office to look for another opportunity to return to Edinburgh. That opportunity came five years later when the Commonwealth Heads of Government Meeting was held at the Palace of Holyroodhouse.

Again, the line-up was impressive. Staying at the Caley were the South African President Nelson Mandela; the Canadian prime minister Jean Chrétien; the prime minister of Pakistan, Muhammed

Singapore's Lee Kuan Yew and wife leaving The Caledonian, while Mr and Mrs Marcos from the Philippines stay for a little bit longer to have their picture taken with some fans.

Following the official presentation and speeches, the Lord Provost invited the South African President to drink a toast from the City of Edinburgh's silver quaich which had been filled with Glenkinchie whisky, a locally distilled single malt. The President was visibly amused, and although a teetotaller, obliged. Having done so he said, 'I'm going to the conference. I hope I'm not too aggressive!'*

** A quaich is a two-handled cup and is the ancient drinking vessel of the Scottish people.*

Naway Sharif; the President of Cyprus, Mr Clerides; the prime minister of Jamaica, Percival J. Patterson; the prime minister of St Kitts & Nevis, Denzil Doulas; the prime minister of Mauritius, Navinchandra Ramgoolan; the prime minister of Singapore, Goh Chok Tong; the President of Sierra Leone, Alhaji Kabbak; Swaziland's head of state, King Mswati III; the President of Tanzania, Beyama William Mkapa, and HRH Prince Tupuoto'a, minister of foreign affairs and defence for Tonga.

'Our stocks have been built up this week with everything from malt whisky to halal meat,' said general manager Steven Carter at the time.

Prince and Princess Michael of Kent

Nelson Mandela's impact on everyone he met was unforgettable. 'I don't care what my room is like so long as I get a good Scottish breakfast in the morning,' he informed staff on arrival. On his departure, he insisted on shaking hands with everybody from the general manager to the front desk receptionist and the hall porter who held the lift door open for him.

And it was during that visit that the Rt Hon Eric Milligan, Lord Provost of the City of Edinburgh, seized the opportunity to present him with the Freedom of the City. Until then, it was unprecedented for this honour not to be handed over in the City Chambers. However, the South African President was staying at the Caledonian Hotel and his schedule was tight. Prime minister Tony Blair had made arrangements for him to visit St Andrews in the afternoon, so it was arranged with Stephen Carter that the ceremony, attended by members of the City Council, would take place immediately after breakfast in the Pompadour Restaurant.

Equally challenging for the staff of the Caley was the gathering that took place in July 1998, when a delegation of Saudi Arabian dignitaries came to celebrate the opening of Edinburgh's new £3.5million mosque at Potterow. They took over dozens of rooms, some of which were set aside for prayer, and required the Caledonian's chefs to display their versatility in preparing a vast selection of special food. It was not a problem. As one might expect, the kitchens of the Caley took it all in their stride.

A Family Arrives

Paul Hampton produced this marvellous shot as part of a Hilton campaign for the cover of the Leisure Breaks magazine autumn 2002/2003.

In 1948 a monumental political change took place that would radically affect the ownership of the Caledonian Hotel. One of the first initiatives of the incoming Labour Government under prime minister Clement Atlee was the nationalisation of the railways to create British Rail, and with this came the formation of a subsidiary company, British Transport Hotels Ltd.

At the time of change-over, Reg Turnbull was appointed general manager, but was succeeded by Addi Jibb in 1950. Everything by then had become a little run-down, and it was part of the challenge of nationalisation that the high standards expected of a top hotel and its staff be revived. Britain as a whole was struggling to get back onto its feet again, and only the best was acceptable.

And by the early 1950s, there was indeed cause to celebrate again, both the Coronation of the young Queen Elizabeth in 1952, and the Caley's half-century, which fell the following year. However, in deference to the climate of austerity that prevailed, such festivities as took place were kept low profile by British Rail. One particularly welcome move, however, was the reinstatement of the upstairs Pompadour Restaurant which re-opened in all of its former glory. This, of course, meant a complete redecoration.

One of the most popular Hollywood stars of her time was Grace Kelly, who was to become Princess Grace of Monaco. The Caledonian was her home in Edinburgh and the staff adored her.

Block Chinese wallpaper and gilt tables were introduced into the foyer, and for the main dining area the colour scheme was lavender, moss green and deep rose. As part of the planned renovation programme, the railings which had originally surrounded the carriageway in front of the hotel were removed and re-erected at Polwarth Tennis Club, on Edinburgh's South Side.

In 1956, the de Guise was closed to make way for Le Postilion, which in turn became The Laird's Lodge. Meanwhile, designers Robert and Roger Nicholson were called in by British Transport Hotels to undertake a full refurbishment. The theme was 'nature' throughout, reflected in the tree motifs of the lounge carpet, silk screened corridors and panels of leaves and flowers. The project took two years to complete, and the designers' names are commemorated in The Nicholson Dining Room, where Roger Nicholson's 230ft hand-painted mural replaced a false ceiling. The canvas had to be painted in a disused post office as Nicholson's studio was too small for the job.

BOAC, for the first time, offered direct flights to Scotland across the Atlantic.

Meanwhile, Britain's economic landscape was changing. Under Dr Beeching, British Rail's Chairman, the transport patterns of the UK were being radically transformed, and the Caledonian Station was just one of the many casualties. In 1964, the Forth Road Bridge, running parallel with the Forth Rail Bridge, had opened up the road to the north to vehicle traffic across the Firth of Forth. At Turnhouse Airport on the outskirts of town, flight traffic was on the increase. As cars and buses increasingly catered to the needs of local commuters, British Rail had already begun the process of re-routing all of its traffic to Waverley Station.

The end of the rail-romance came on 6 September 1965, when the Caledonian Station was finally closed down. The popular Oyster Bar which had opened off Platform 7 went out of business. It was under the management of Albert Smith, and its unexpected speciality was prawn cocktails. Les Murphy, a young cocktail shaker in the American Bar became so well known for his conversation and wit that some guests used to call it 'Murphy's Bar.'

For many, particularly those who made everyday use of the local lines, the demise of the Caledonian Station was cause for great sadness. As a schoolboy, Eric Milligan, later to become the city's Lord Provost, regularly travelled into town by train from Merchiston. 'People living in the west looked at it as the gateway into the city,' he said. And thereafter, for five years, the site remained unused, with the exception of one memorable occasion when it was taken over by Edinburgh's French community to celebrate Bastille Day.

In 1970, having built the splendid Meadowbank Stadium and the Royal Commonwealth Pool on Dalkeith Road, Edinburgh hosted the British Commonwealth Games. Recognising that visitor traffic was definitely on the increase again, British Transport Hotels decided that it was time to enlarge, and instructed an addition to be made of a new wing containing fifty one more bedrooms on the upper three floors. The building's V-shaped plan, with Lothian Road and Rutland Street forming the legs, changed to an A-shape.

In 1971, the Lothian Lounge was built on the site of the former station's booking office, and the entire development took up the area formerly occupied by the station platforms. For some of those who had fond memories of the station in the old days, it came as a shock to find themselves indoors when they had previously been outside. Edinburgh-based playwright A J Stewart, for example, found it strangely surreal to drink cocktails under one of the Caledonian Railway Company coats-of-arms when she had previously used it as a meeting point for meeting friends on the platform when travelling.

In April 1978, Her Majesty the Queen officially opened the enlarged Edinburgh Airport close to the original site at Turnhouse. On 21 December, the Caley's 75th anniversary was commemorated with considerably more style than its 50th.

Staff dressed in turn-of-the-century costume stepped out into Edinburgh's snowy West End to hand out cups of mulled wine and mince pies to passers by. A souvenir menu was drawn up featuring King Edward VII's favourite Sunday luncheon dish, an Edwardian speciality – *Alois de boeuf anglais*, and *Aiguilettes de caneton à l'orange*.

The Caley's head barman, Charlie 'Duff' Duffy created a cocktail called '1903' consisting of Scotch whisky, beaten egg, heather honey and lemon juice. It cost 75p. A more lasting tribute, in the form of a cherry tree, was planted in nearby Rutland Square Gardens by the Lord Provost, Sir Kenneth Borthwick.

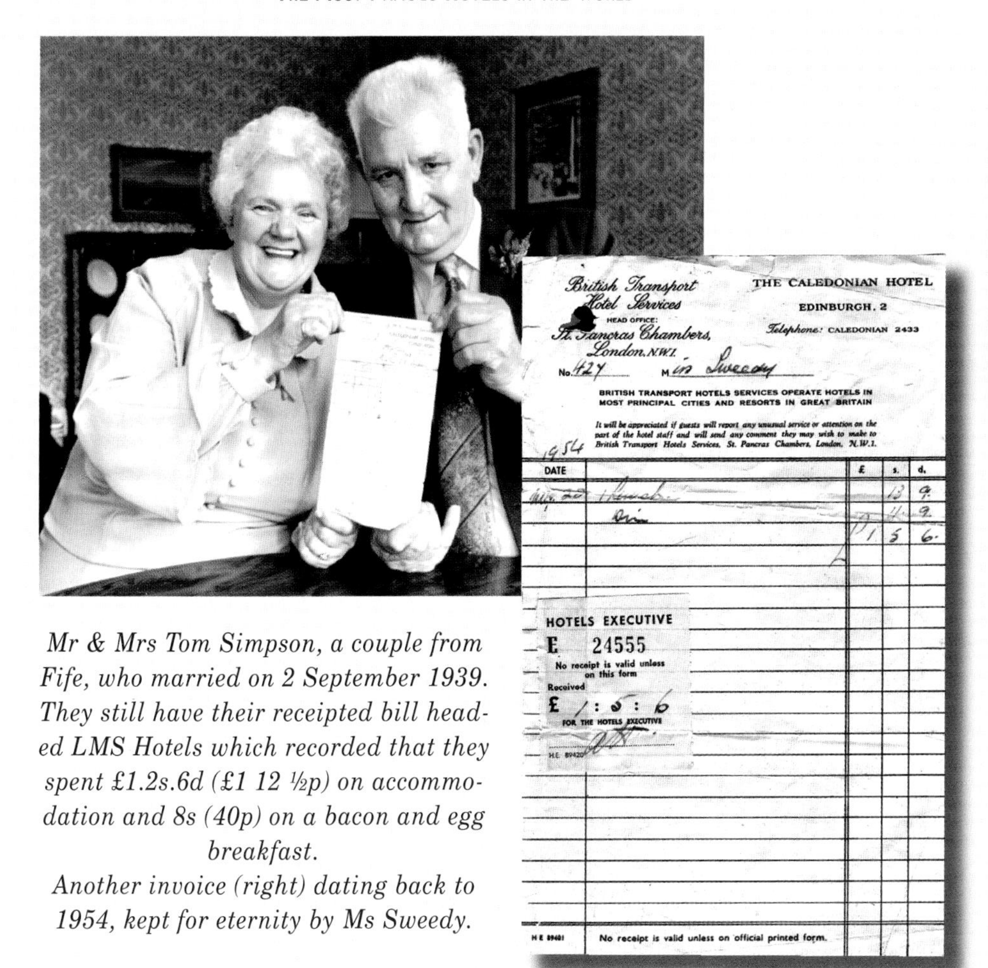

British Transport Hotel Services
HEAD OFFICE:
St. Pancras Chambers,
London, N.W.1.

THE CALEDONIAN HOTEL
EDINBURGH. 2
Telephone: CALEDONIAN 2433

No. 427 M iss Sweedy

BRITISH TRANSPORT HOTELS SERVICES OPERATE HOTELS IN MOST PRINCIPAL CITIES AND RESORTS IN GREAT BRITAIN

It will be appreciated if guests will report any unusual service or attention on the part of the hotel staff and will send any comment they may wish to make to British Transport Hotels Services, St. Pancras Chambers, London, N.W.1.

1954

DATE		£	s.	d.
			13	9
			4	9
		1	5	6

HOTELS EXECUTIVE
E 24555
No receipt is valid unless on this form
Received
£ 1 : 5 : 6
FOR THE HOTELS EXECUTIVE
H.E. 89420

H.E. 89401 No receipt is valid unless on official printed form.

Mr & Mrs Tom Simpson, a couple from Fife, who married on 2 September 1939. They still have their receipted bill headed LMS Hotels which recorded that they spent £1.2s.6d (£1 12 ½p) on accommodation and 8s (40p) on a bacon and egg breakfast.
Another invoice (right) dating back to 1954, kept for eternity by Ms Sweedy.

Successful grand hotels in many ways operate as one big happy family and the Caley has always looked after its own, annually inviting staff back for regular visits long after they have ceased to be employed there. But then loyalty works both ways: Joan Learmonth came to the hotel in the 1980s for a six-week trial in banqueting, and stayed for ten years. 'There were 400 staff in those days,' she recalled. 'But everybody knew your name.'

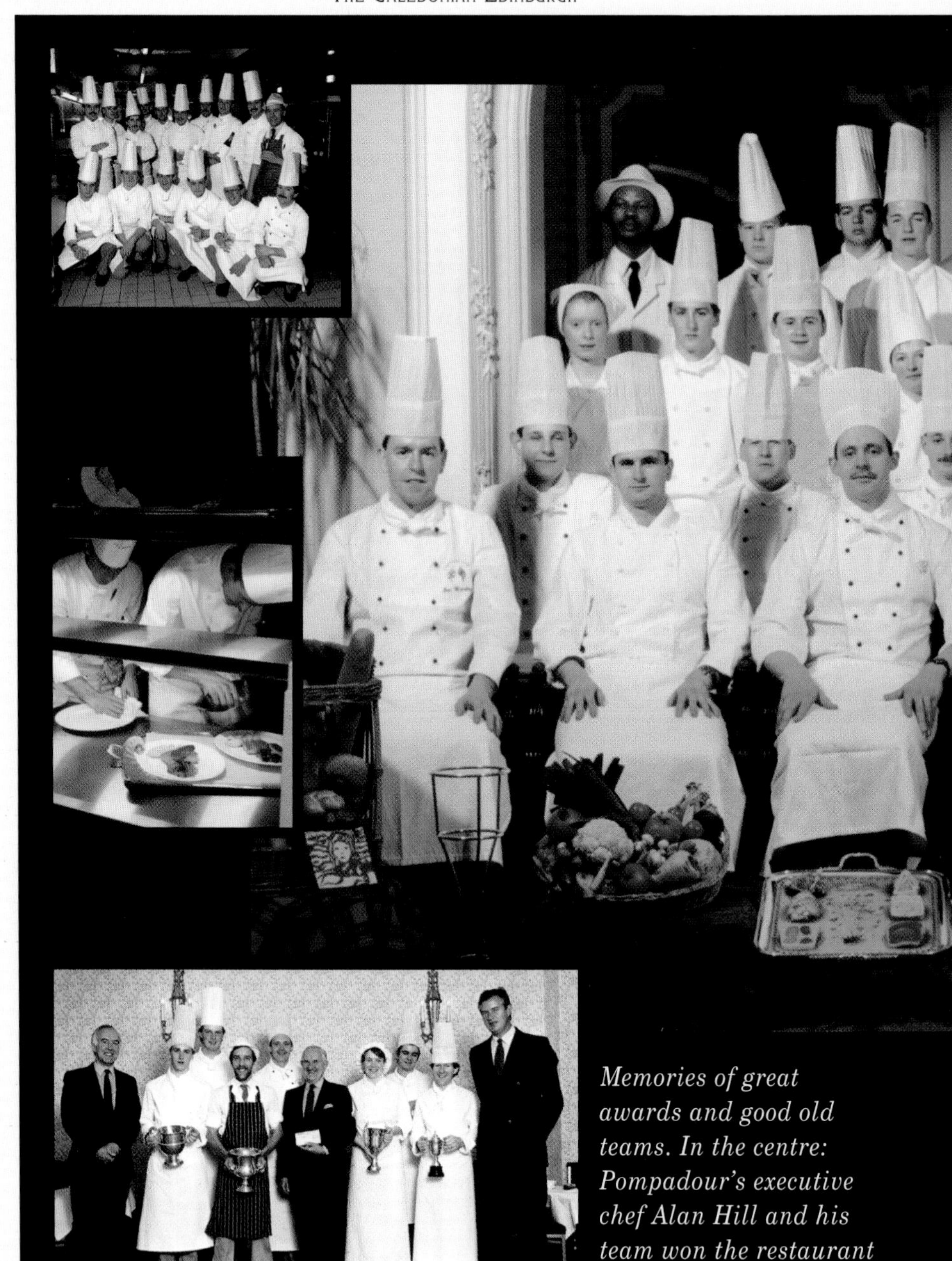

Memories of great awards and good old teams. In the centre: Pompadour's executive chef Alan Hill and his team won the restaurant the coveted AA Rosette (1985).

Luncheon

Melon Frappé

Soufflé de Turbotin Grimaldi

Poulet en Cocotte aux Primeurs
Haricots Verts Fines Herbes
Pommes Nouvelles au Beurre

Poire Glacée Juliette
Gourmandises

Café

Caledonian Hotel
Edinburgh

1st September 1955

Close–Ups

The Staff

It's the People . . . Now and Then

The Caledonian has five kitchens, 29 chefs, 202 ch

1993: general manager David Clarke, resident manager Lynn Abernethy and staff.

TS, TWO MILES OF CORRIDOR CARPETING, 1,200 STEPS AND

Close–Ups

The Staff

Caledonian guests consume 5,000 bottles of champagne

2003: general manager Dagmar Mühle and some awarded members of the staff.

:AR. 100,000 EGGS AND 18,000 GALLONS OF MILK ARE USED.

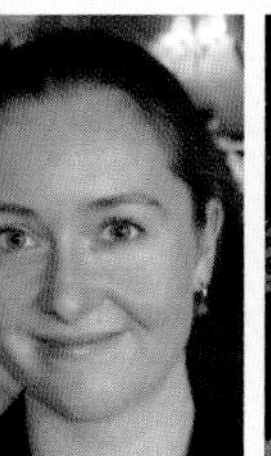

Close-Ups

THE STAFF

6.6 MILLION GALLONS OF WATER ARE GOING DOWN TH

N WHILE MORE THAN 11,000 LIGHT BULBS SHINE ON.

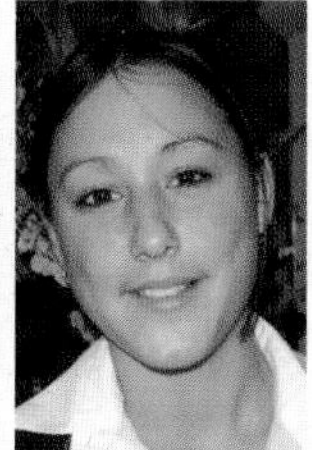

Rules for staff were strict. The basement porter started organising the coal fires at 3.30am. An Irish housekeeper called Miss Kelly ruled the chambermaids with a rod of iron. Even the managers deferred to her. 'They're my girls,' she would inform them. 'I do the telling off, but never in front of anybody else.'

And there was certainly no room for staff romance. Stewart Scoular, for example, met his wife Ruth when she was a receptionist at the hotel, and she had to leave her job when they decided to marry in 1960.

For Sarah Callaghan, who became the hotel's business yield manager during the 1980s, it was simpler. She joined the Caledonian's staff on a placement from a Cardiff hotel college during the 1980s. She had intended to go to Zurich, 'but I was being guided by some unknown hand,' she said. On her very first day, she was sent from Reception to Reservations on the first floor and lost her way. As she passed the Pompadour, a handsome waiter appeared and offered to accompany her. 'He has been accompanying me ever since,' she said, referring to her husband Gerry, who went on to run a hotel recruitment company.

Loyalties and memories linger on among the public too, many of whom remember being taken to tea there as children. The lavish afternoon teas were served on silver cake stands laden with smoked salmon, ham, cheese and cucumber sandwiches, and there were cakes and scones served with lashings of jam and clotted cream. It was the ultimate treat.

And generations of schoolboys, including the co-author of this book, had their hair cut by the Caledonian's barber, Jack Hunter, or 'Mr Hunter' as he was more usually addressed. Originally, the shop opened off the station and occupied a room that was later used as a luggage store. Later it moved into the hotel itself, downstairs, below the lounge.

'He seemed to know everyone in Edinburgh, if not in Scotland,'

GM Alan Blest and Harry Clair

GM Steven Carter and Billy Garioch

GM David Clarke and Gavin Binnie

GM Fitzpatrick and Harry Wheatcroft

GM Dagmar Mühle and team celebrating the '1–5 years of service-award'.

Recognition is always welcome, be it a handshake, a golden watch or the pin-badge for one year of service with the Caledonian.

PUFFINS

Sir Iain Moncreiffe of that Ilk

Among the private luncheon clubs which met at the Caley during the early 1970s was Puffins. During the early 1970s Sir Iain Moncreiffe of that Ilk, who was often unfairly described in the newspapers as Britain's greatest snob, founded Puffins. Sir Iain, who held the heraldic post of Unicorn Pursuivant at the Court of the Lord Lyon King of Arms, would express an immediate interest in the ancestry of anybody he met. It was simply his interest in genealogy that prompted this, not affectation, and as a result he gathered around him an eclectic mix of acquaintances ranging from commoners to kings. Impeccably well-mannered, the 'Ilk', as he was affectionately known, treated everyone, including the staff who served in the private dining room, with exceptional courtesy.

Puffins was originally launched during the 1950s at L'Aperitif Restaurant in Frederick Street, exclusively for individuals who lived outside the city but who came to town on a Wednesday either on business or to shop. With a male-only membership that included King Zog of Albania and actor Terence Stamp, any member who looked in for a bite of lunch on a Wednesday would not expect, or be expected to leave the table much before late afternoon. In the interim period, he or she (ladies could be brought along as guests) would be regally entertained by many of Scotland's leading writers, politicians, and such legal luminaries as the great Edinburgh raconteur Lionel Daiches QC, and Sir Nicholas Fairbairn, a one-time Solicitor General for Scotland, renowned for his flamboyant lifestyle.

observed a regular client. 'It was by appointment only, and you often had to book a week or more in advance, unless he knew you particularly well. But the days of 'short back and sides' were coming to an end, and hair salons were springing up all over town. When Mr Hunter retired, it truly was the end of an era.

On 22 June 1980, British Transport Hotels was broken up. The Conservative Government under Margaret Thatcher was determined to introduce privatisation wherever possible, so a new company was formed to incorporate and run The Gleneagles Hotel and golf courses in Perthshire, and the North British Hotel and Caledonian Hotel in Edinburgh. It was called The Gleneagles Hotels Public Limited Company and attracted investment from a number of major life assurance companies, pension funds and financial institutions.

William T. Stevenson from the Scottish Transport Group was the Chairman, and Chief Executive Peter Tyrie and Marketing Director Peter Bates led the management team. Both Tyrie and Bates were eventually to move on to major and equally remarkable hotel and tourism enterprises in the years that followed.

However, in the short term, their impact on the entire ethos of hotels in Scotland was breathtaking. Over the next three years, a spectacular £5 million programme of improvements took place, with the Caley accounting for approximately half of the investment. On 11 October 1983, city dignitaries, clients and friends were invited to inspect the results at a lavish champagne reception. A small booklet entitled *The First Eighty Years* was commissioned from writer Jeremy Bruce-Watt.

Nine years earlier, in an article in 'The Chicago Tribune', Horace Sutton had described the Caley as 'Pitch black on the outside and pumpkin

Under one roof for a short while: The Gleneagles Hotel and the Caledonian

Close-ups

Development

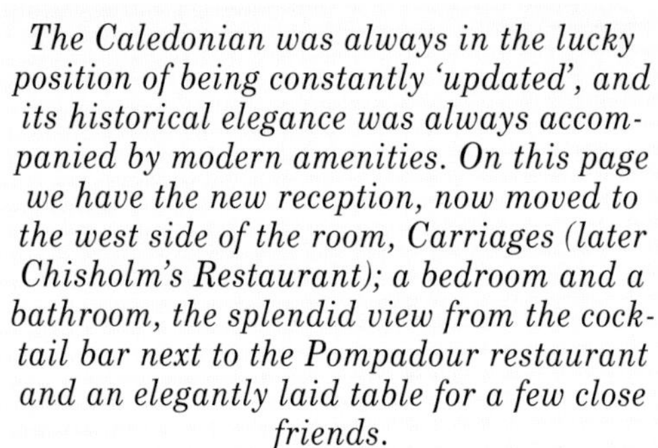

The Caledonian was always in the lucky position of being constantly 'updated', and its historical elegance was always accompanied by modern amenities. On this page we have the new reception, now moved to the west side of the room, Carriages (later Chisholm's Restaurant); a bedroom and a bathroom, the splendid view from the cocktail bar next to the Pompadour restaurant and an elegantly laid table for a few close friends.

bright in the lounge.' It was time to wash away the exterior grime of almost seventy years and reveal the blush pink of the stone beneath. Following restoration of the red sandstone, the entire hotel was double glazed.

Paying homage to the style of the past, the mahogany and glass revolving door from the 1930s was re-installed at the main entrance. A second revolving door was introduced to the right of it to provide access to the adjoining Pullman Lounge, a quiet and spacious bar area much frequented by local business folk.

Simultaneously, the reception area was moved from the east to the west side of the entrance hall, where it remains. The interior decoration work was carried out by Ezra Attia of London, who sensibly retained many of the features introduced by the Nicholson brothers, in particular the tree motif on the balustrade of the grand staircase and the huge chandelier which hangs above it.

The original dining room with Roger Nicholson's golden eagle mural and its outlook to the east became the Castle Suite, catering for large gatherings of up to 200 guests, a popular ballroom for countless wedding receptions, dinner dances, and such events as Edinburgh's annual Christmas Charity Ball, a great favourite with the city's young socialites.

The hotel lounge, with its imposing Grecian columns, continued to serve traditional afternoon teas. Adjoining (where once had been the de Guise) was The Gazebo, a brasserie/grill style restaurant for breakfast and late night snacks, open to non-residents and providing a self-service buffet at lunch time.

In 1990, the previous open grill was converted into a totally modern kitchen area and the restaurant re-named Carriages, with a dance floor and capacity for 155 guests. Another innovation was to provide The Gazebo and the lounge with an outlook onto a flower garden which is floodlit at night.

To the right of the top of the grand staircase, the Pompadour Restaurant remained in place. Although re-carpeted, the Louis XV décor was retained. A pianist still plays nightly, and a small band

entertains on Friday and Saturday nights. A portrait of Madame de Pompadour looks benignly over the adjoining cocktail bar which is enclosed with heavy pink marble screens and guarded by gilt lions. On the same floor are the Versailles Room, with walls painted to represent the gardens of the Palace of Versailles, and the Trianon Room, whose name derives from the Grand and Petit Trianons of the gardens of Versailles. Then there are the smaller Montrose and Atholl suites, the latter incorporating the Rannoch, Tummel and Tay rooms, largely in demand for private commercial functions. For a time, the mirrored ballroom, which featured Nicholson's militaria centrepiece, one of his less successful creations, was retained for wedding receptions and small private dances, but the space has since been transformed into three business suites – the Glamis, Dornoch and Braemar.

Fifty additional bedrooms were also added to the fifth floor, bringing the hotel's total today up to 249. The telephone operators (almost) lost their 'can you please get me . . .' job, as direct-dial telephones were installed throughout. In 1984, Gleneagles Hotels PLC was acquired by Scotch whisky distiller Arthur Bell & Sons PLC, and in 1986, with the Gleneagles Hotel remaining under the ownership of United Distillers, the North British Hotel was sold to a company set up with Peter Tyrie as managing director, and re-named The Balmoral Hotel. Meanwhile, the 5-star Caledonian Hotel, with Alan Blest as general manager, was acquired by Norfolk Capital Hotels. Alan moved to the St James's Club in 1989, and was replaced by David Clarke, who remained in place when the Caley was sold to Queens Moat Houses PLC in 1990.

Facilities were added: a swimming pool on the lower ground floor, a health club, spa, Jacuzzi and sauna.

General manager Steven Carter celebrates the opening of Henry J Bean's with the Lord and Lady Provost, Linda Murray and Edinburgh Evening News *columnist John Gibson.*

A traditional pub bar called Platform One (later Henry J Bean's Bar and Grill) was opened, with public access from Rutland Street only.

In 1986, Edinburgh once again hosted the Royal Commonwealth Games, which provided a boost to the Scottish tourist industry. Edinburgh Council also embarked upon the promotion of a further series of festivals to attract more all-year-round visitors to the capital. The Edinburgh Science Festival takes place in April, and Edinburgh's week long Hogmanay celebrations culminate in a spectacular firework display from Edinburgh Castle on New Year's Eve.

It was a triumphant period for the hotel, with a succession of chefs of the calibre of Allan Hill, Paul Rogerson, Jeff Bland, Tony Binks and Graeme Cockburn. Having been awarded an AA Rosette in 1985, the Pompadour was in 1988 nominated the best restaurant in Scotland by Decanter Magazine, sponsored by Macallan, and the Taste of Scotland Scheme, sponsored by Caithness Glass. The Caledonian Hotel itself was nominated the best hotel in Scotland by the Scottish Tourist Board in 1989 and 1990.

From January to 1 March 1991, rooms 200, 202, 204 and 236 were leased as temporary office accommodation for the Consulate General of Japan while arrangements were made for a new Edinburgh office in Melville Street. The increase in the number of Japanese guests visiting Scotland and the appearance of the first Japanese Consulate outside London was no doubt influenced by the fact that 18 major Japanese companies were operating in Scotland by then. It was at this stage that some members of the Caley's staff were encouraged to attend seminars in Japanese language and culture.

And despite the eight per cent drop in overseas tourism experienced throughout Scotland in the aftermath of the Gulf War, the Caley persevered in providing only the best. In 1992, the Pompadour was once again voted *Taste of Scotland's* Restaurant of the Year. The following year, Caley headwaiter Riccardo Zanetti was a finalist in the Remy Martin Head Waiter of the Year Award. And keeping pace with the times, fax lines and personal computer lines were introduced into all of the bedrooms.

In July 1993, the month of Edinburgh's Royal garden parties, the Caley celebrated its 90th birthday with another small booklet on its history, this time entitled *Luxury Edinburgh* and written by *Edinburgh Evening News* journalist Ian Nimmo. Champagne and strawberries were served at an 'Alternative' Garden Party hosted by David Clarke in the hotel's Gazebo Gardens, to the sound of a string quartet. To launch a scheme aimed at encouraging the planting of trees to commemorate special occasions, the Rt Hon Norman Irons, the Lord Provost; Willie Samuel, the City Council's Vice-Convenor, and Caledonian general manager David Clarke planted ten oaks to mark the event.

David Clarke left the Caley in 1994 and Stephen Carter took over as general manager. In June 1998, it was decided to change the name of Carriages Restaurant to Chisholm's Restaurant to give diners an association with an individual historic figure. Jazz fans might be forgiven for assuming

Caley Nessie

Hilton

After Hilton has taken over in 2000, Hilton Group chief executive officer David Michels honoured back of the house manager Angela Doyle as 'the employee of the year'.

the name honours the Scots trombonist-comedian George Chisholm, but it was in fact a tribute to Professor George G. Chisholm (1850-1930) who became Scotland's first professor of Geography at Edinburgh University in 1908. As a regular visitor to the hotel, it was generally felt that there was bond between him and the hotel's international reputation and transport links.

In March 2000, the Caledonian Hotel was acquired by Hilton Hotels PLC. It was a new beginning for a new millennium as the great old Edinburgh landmark began its stately approach to its 100th birthday, guided by Dagmar Mühle, the first woman to hold the post of general manager since our story began.

In 2000, Hilton made The Caledonian their flagship in Scotland

Caledonian Hilton
CHISHOLMS

DUGALD

A Capital Reborn

In 1999, after almost 300 years, Edinburgh once again became home to a Scottish Parliament. The original Scottish Parliament was dissolved in 1707 following the Act of Union which created a London-based United Kingdom parliament to represent England, Scotland, Ireland and Wales. Since then, devolved government was an ongoing debate, but in a referendum held in 1998, the people of both Scotland and Wales voted for more localised control over their own affairs.

The outcome of this was particularly significant for Edinburgh which has since come into its own, not only as Scotland's capital, but as an international destination. Prior to 1995, the centre was designated a World Heritage Site by UNESCO, so the status was already in place. Now it has been confirmed, and the city is prospering as never before. The population is growing steadily, there is an unprecedented rush of new building, and property prices are flourishing.

The city's West End was the first beneficiary of this new-found optimism. Behind the Cale-

Left page top and clockwise: Edinburgh looking west from Calton Hill; Hopetoun House, 18th century collaborative masterpiece of the architects William and Robert Adam; A train crossing the Forth Bridge; The Royal Yacht Britannia at the Ocean Terminal; A statue in Leith by Lucy Poett of Sandy Irvine Robertson (1942–1999), a well-known local businessman and benefactor who was a regular patron of the Caley.

donian Hotel, on either side of Lothian Road, there have been extensive developments encompassing Festival Square, the rotunda of the Edinburgh International Conference Centre, and Edinburgh's business quarter. On Castle Terrace, Saltire Court incorporates the avant garde Traverse Theatre complex, in close proximity to its older neighbours, the Usher Hall and the Royal Lyceum Theatre.

Thus the old and the new are blended together with finesse. Elsewhere in the city, the Royal Scottish Academy at the far end of Princes Street has undergone a renovation, and behind it is the National Gallery of Scotland. There is the splendid Scottish National Portrait Gallery on George Street, and the Scottish National Gallery of Modern Art and its sister, the Dean Gallery, on Belford Road, all within walking distance from the West End. On the Royal Mile is the Scotch Whisky Heritage Centre, close to the Royal Museum and Museum of Scotland in Chambers Street.

Retailing has also had a boost with the arrival of upmarket fashion retailer Harvey Nichols in St Andrew Square, and regeneration has gone beyond the city centre. At Holyrood, overlooked by Salisbury Crags and the height known as Arthur's Seat, is the purpose built Scottish Parliament complex. In close proximity to the Parliament is Our Dynamic Earth, built in 1999. This takes visitors on a thrilling journey through the planet and solar system.

From the Pentland Hills, trickling through Edinburgh is the Water of Leith, a "ribbon of green" that passes through the urban villages of Colinton, Murrayfield and Stockbridge to emerge at Leith Docks on the Firth of Forth. Here, beside designer Sir Terence Conran's Ocean Terminal with its shopping malls and cinema complexes, is anchored the de-commissioned Royal Yacht Britannia, a major visitor attraction.

The Caledonian Hotel's pivotal position at the very heart of Edinburgh has always been its greatest asset, and never more so than now. Under the enlightened ownership of Hilton, a £15 million refurbishment is to take place over the coming two years, commencing with a full upgrade of the de luxe rooms, relocation of en suite bathrooms, and the installation of air conditioning throughout.

The Caley was built as a bold Edwardian counterpoint to the city's magnificent classical Georgian architecture which was inspired by award-winning architect James Craig in the late 1700s. Today the hotel's blush-red Permian sandstone façade, and what is to be found behind it, is no less inspirational to successive generations. Created out of the 19th century railway boom, this great 5-star palace of hospitality is facing the future with both confidence and pride in its ability to keep pace with the times. The accolade of "Luxury Edinburgh" is as justified now as it was when it all began.

FIN

The view from the Royal Suite.

Epilogue

Once again we are packing our suitcases. Room-service brings up the breakfast. One last view of Edinburgh Castle over the coffee cup. Now the porters are knocking for the luggage. I leave the hotel through the revolving door.

Once again, my mind travels back to the days when steam engines pulled their heavy loads along the tracks of the Caledonian Railway. Did I just hear the whistle of a locomotive? Ah no, it's Charlie, hailing a taxi.

Fraser's corner and the 1930s revolving door, reinstalled in the 1980s.

Helpful hands put the luggage and all the rest in the cab. A Caledonian teddy bear changes owner at the last minute – the little chap is obviously looking forward to the journey ahead.

We say our farewells and know that we will miss our friends at *The Caley*. The exquisite food at the Pompadour, the friendly people all over the hotel who have helped us to make our stay such an enjoyable one . . .

But we also know that once we leave we are already on our way back. That helps – and the journey continues.

Caledonian Teddy;
Billy Garioch and Charlie Rodger.